JAMESTOWN  EDUCA

Timed Readings Plus
in Social Studies

BOOK 6

**25 Two-Part Lessons with Questions for
Building Reading Speed and Comprehension**

 **Glencoe**

New York, New York   Columbus, Ohio   Chicago, Illinois   Peoria, Illinois   Woodland Hills, California

JAMESTOWN EDUCATION

Glencoe

The McGraw·Hill Companies

ISBN: 0-07-845804-8

Send all queries to:
Glencoe/McGraw-Hill
8787 Orion Place
Columbus, OH 43240-4027

2 3 4 5 6 7 8 9 10 021 08 07 06 05 04

CONTENTS

To the Student

    Reading Faster and Better   2

    Mastering Reading Comprehension   3

    Working Through a Lesson   7

    Plotting Your Progress   8

To the Teacher

    About the Series   9

    Timed Reading and Comprehension   10

    Speed Versus Comprehension   10

    Getting Started   10

    Timing the Reading   11

    Teaching a Lesson   11

    Monitoring Progress   12

    Diagnosis and Evaluation   12

Lessons   13–112

Answer Key   114–115

Graphs   116–118

TO THE STUDENT

You probably talk at an average rate of about 150 words a minute. If you are a reader of average ability, you read at a rate of about 250 words a minute. So your reading speed is nearly twice as fast as your speaking or listening speed. This example shows that reading is one of the fastest ways to get information.

The purpose of this book is to help you increase your reading rate and understand what you read. The 25 lessons in this book will also give you practice in reading social studies articles and in preparing for tests in which you must read and understand nonfiction passages within a certain time limit.

Reading Faster and Better

Following are some strategies that you can use to read the articles in each lesson.

Previewing

Previewing before you read is a very important step. This helps you to get an idea of what a selection is about and to recall any previous knowledge you have about the subject. Here are the steps to follow when previewing.

Read the title. Titles are designed not only to announce the subject but also to make the reader think. Ask yourself questions such as What can I learn from the title? What thoughts does it bring to mind?

What do I already know about this subject?

Read the first sentence. If they are short, read the first two sentences. The opening sentence is the writer's opportunity to get your attention. Some writers announce what they hope to tell you in the selection. Some writers state their purpose for writing; others just try to get your attention.

Read the last sentence. If it is short, read the final two sentences. The closing sentence is the writer's last chance to get ideas across to you. Some writers repeat the main idea once more. Some writers draw a conclusion—this is what they have been leading up to. Other writers summarize their thoughts; they tie all the facts together.

Skim the entire selection. Glance through the selection quickly to see what other information you can pick up. Look for anything that will help you read fluently and with understanding. Are there names, dates, or numbers? If so, you may have to read more slowly.

Reading for Meaning

Here are some ways to make sure you are making sense of what you read.

Build your concentration. You cannot understand what you read if you are not concentrating. When you discover that your thoughts are straying, correct the situation right away. Avoid distractions and distracting situations. Keep in mind the information you learned from previewing. This will help focus your attention on the selection.

Read in thought groups. Try to see meaningful combinations of words—phrases, clauses, or sentences. If you look at only one word at a time (called word-by-word reading), both your comprehension and your reading speed suffer.

Ask yourself questions. To sustain the pace you have set for yourself and to maintain a high level of concentration and comprehension, ask yourself questions such as What does this mean? or How can I use this information? as you read.

Finding the Main Ideas

The paragraph is the basic unit of meaning. If you can quickly discover and understand the main idea of each paragraph, you will build your comprehension of the selection.

Find the topic sentence. The topic sentence, which contains the main idea, often is the first sentence of a paragraph. It is followed by sentences that support, develop, or explain the main idea. Sometimes a topic sentence comes at the end of a paragraph. When it does, the supporting details come first, building the base for the topic sentence. Some paragraphs do not have a topic sentence; all of the sentences combine to create a meaningful idea.

Understand paragraph structure. Every well-written paragraph has a purpose. The purpose may be to inform, define, explain, or illustrate. The purpose should always relate to the main idea and expand on it. As you read each paragraph, see how the body of the paragraph tells you more about the main idea.

Relate ideas as you read. As you read the selection, notice how the writer puts together ideas. As you discover the relationship between the ideas, the main ideas come through quickly and clearly.

Mastering Reading Comprehension

Reading fast is not useful if you don't remember or understand what you read. The two exercises in Part A provide a check on how well you have understood the article.

Recalling Facts

These multiple-choice questions provide a quick check to see how well you recall important information from the article. As you learn to apply the reading strategies described earlier, you should be able to answer these questions more successfully.

Understanding Ideas

These questions require you to think about the main ideas in the article. Some main ideas are stated in the article; others are not. To answer some of the questions, you need to draw conclusions about what you read.

The five exercises in Part B require multiple answers. These exercises provide practice in applying comprehension and critical thinking skills that you can use in all your reading.

Recognizing Words in Context

Always check to see whether the words around an unfamiliar word—its context—can give you a clue to the word's meaning. A word generally appears in a context related to its meaning.

Suppose, for example, that you are unsure of the meaning of the word *expired* in the following passage:

> Vera wanted to check out a book, but her library card had expired. She had to borrow my card, because she didn't have time to renew hers.

You could begin to figure out the meaning of *expired* by asking yourself a question such as, What could have happened to Vera's library card that would make her need to borrow someone else's card? You might realize that if Vera had to renew her card, its usefulness must have come to an end or run out. This would lead you to conclude that the word *expired* must mean "to come to an end" or "to run out." You would be right. The context suggested the meaning.

Context can also affect the meaning of a word you already know. The word *key,* for instance, has many meanings. There are musical keys, door keys, and keys to solving a mystery. The context in which the word *key* occurs will tell you which meaning is correct.

Sometimes a word is explained by the words that immediately follow it. The subject of a sentence and your knowledge about that subject might also help you determine the meaning of an unknown word. Try to decide the meaning of the word *revive* in the following sentence:

> Sunshine and water will revive those drooping plants.

The compound subject is *sunshine* and *water.* You know that plants need light and water to survive and that drooping plants are not healthy. You can figure out that *revive* means "to bring back to health."

Distinguishing Fact from Opinion

Every day you are called upon to sort out fact and opinion. Because much of what you read and hear contains both facts and opinions, you need to be able to tell the two apart.

Facts are statements that can be proved. The proof must be objective and verifiable. You must be able to check for yourself to confirm a fact.

Look at the following facts. Notice that they can be checked for accuracy and confirmed. Suggested sources for verification appear in parentheses.

- Abraham Lincoln was the 16th president of the United States. (Consult biographies, social studies books, encyclopedias, and similar sources.)

- Earth revolves around the Sun. (Research in encyclopedias or astronomy books; ask knowledgeable people.)
- Dogs walk on four legs. (See for yourself.)

Opinions are statements that cannot be proved. There is no objective evidence you can consult to check the truthfulness of an opinion. Unlike facts, opinions express personal beliefs or judgments. Opinions reveal how someone feels about a subject, not the facts about that subject. You might agree or disagree with someone's opinion, but you cannot prove it right or wrong.

Look at the following opinions. The reasons these statements are classified as opinions appear in parentheses.

- Abraham Lincoln was born to be a president. (You cannot prove this by referring to birth records. There is no evidence to support this belief.)
- Earth is the only planet in our solar system where intelligent life exists. (There is no proof of this. It may be proved true some day, but for now it is just an educated guess—not a fact.)
- The dog is a human's best friend. (This is not a fact; your best friend might not be a dog.)

As you read, be aware that facts and opinions are often mixed together. Both are useful to you as a reader. But to evaluate what you read and to read intelligently, you need to know the difference between the two.

Keeping Events in Order

Sequence, or chronological order, is the order of events in a story or article or the order of steps in a process. Paying attention to the sequence of events or steps will help you follow what is happening, predict what might happen next, and make sense of a passage.

To make the sequence as clear as possible, writers often use signal words to help the reader get a more exact idea of when things happen. Following is a list of frequently used signal words and phrases:

until	first
next	then
before	after
finally	later
when	while
during	now
at the end	by the time
as soon as	in the beginning

Signal words and phrases are also useful when a writer chooses to relate details or events out of sequence. You need to pay careful attention to determine the correct chronological order.

Making Correct Inferences

Much of what you read *suggests* more than it *says*. Writers often do not state ideas directly in a text. They can't. Think of the time and space it would take to state every idea. And think of how boring that would be! Instead, writers leave it to you, the reader, to fill in the information they leave out—to make inferences. You do this by combining clues in the story or article with knowledge from your own experience.

You make many inferences every day. Suppose, for example, that you are visiting a friend's house for the first time. You see a bag of kitty litter. You infer (make an inference) that the family has a cat. Another day you overhear a conversation. You catch the names of two actors and the words *scene, dialogue,* and *directing.* You infer that the people are discussing a movie or play.

In these situations and others like them, you infer unstated information from what you observe or read. Readers must make inferences in order to understand text.

Be careful about the inferences you make. One set of facts may suggest several inferences. Some of these inferences could be faulty. A correct inference must be supported by evidence.

Remember that bag of kitty litter that caused you to infer that your friend has a cat? That could be a faulty inference. Perhaps your friend's family uses the kitty litter on their icy sidewalks to create traction. To be sure your inference is correct, you need more evidence.

Understanding Main Ideas

The main idea is the most important idea in a paragraph or passage—the idea that provides purpose and direction. The rest of the selection explains, develops, or supports the main idea. Without a main idea, there would be only a collection of unconnected thoughts.

In the following paragraph, the main idea is printed in italics. As you read, observe how the other sentences develop or explain the main idea.

Typhoon Chris hit with full fury today on the central coast of Japan. Heavy rain from the storm flooded the area. High waves carried many homes into the sea. People now fear that the heavy rains will cause mudslides in the central part of the country. The number of people killed by the storm may climb past the 200 mark by Saturday.

In this paragraph, the main-idea statement appears first. It is followed by sentences that explain, support, or give details. Sometimes the main idea appears at the end of a paragraph. Writers often put the main idea at the end of a paragraph when their purpose is to persuade or convince. Readers may be more open to a new idea if the reasons for it are presented first.

As you read the following paragraph, think about the overall impact of the supporting ideas. Their purpose is to convince the reader that the main idea in the last sentence should be accepted.

Last week there was a head-on collision at Huntington and Canton streets. Just a month ago a pedestrian was struck there. Fortunately, she was only slightly injured. In the past year, there have been more accidents there than at any other corner in the city. In fact, nearly 10 percent of all accidents in the city occur at the corner. This intersection is very dangerous, and a traffic signal should be installed there before a life is lost.

The details in the paragraph progress from least important to most important. They achieve their full effect in the main idea statement at the end.

In many cases, the main idea is not expressed in a single sentence. The reader is called upon to interpret all of the ideas expressed in the paragraph and to decide upon a main idea. Read the following paragraph.

> The American author Jack London was once a pupil at the Cole Grammar School in Oakland, California. Each morning the class sang a song. When the teacher noticed that Jack wouldn't sing, she sent him to the principal. He returned to class with a note. The note said that Jack could be excused from singing with the class if he would write an essay every morning.

In this paragraph, the reader has to interpret the individual ideas and to decide on a main idea. This main idea seems reasonable: Jack London's career as a writer began with a punishment in grammar school.

Understanding the concept of the main idea and knowing how to find it is important. Transferring that understanding to your reading and study is also important.

Working Through a Lesson

Part A

1. **Preview the article.** Locate the timed selection in Part A of the lesson that you are going to read. Wait for your teacher's signal to preview. You will have 20 seconds for previewing. Follow the previewing steps described on page 2.

2. **Read the article.** When your teacher gives you the signal, begin reading. Read carefully so that you will be able to answer questions about what you have read. When you finish reading, look at the board and note your reading time. Write this time at the bottom of the page on the line labeled Reading Time.

3. **Complete the exercises.** Answer the 10 questions that follow the article. There are 5 fact questions and 5 idea questions. Choose the best answer to each question and put an X in that box.

4. **Correct your work.** Use the Answer Key at the back of the book to check your answers. Circle any wrong answer and put an X in the box you should have marked. Record the number of correct answers on the appropriate line at the end of the lesson.

Part B

1. **Preview and read the passage.** Use the same techniques you

used to read Part A. Think about what you are reading.

2. **Complete the exercises.** Instructions are given for answering each category of question. There are 15 responses for you to record.

3. **Correct your work.** Use the Answer Key at the back of the book. Circle any wrong answer and write the correct letter or number next to it. Record the number of correct answers on the appropriate line at the end of the lesson.

Plotting Your Progress

1. **Find your reading rate.** Turn to the Reading Rate graph on page 116. Put an X at the point where the vertical line that represents the lesson intersects your reading time, shown along the left-hand side. The right-hand side of the graph will reveal your words-per-minute reading speed.

2. **Find your comprehension score.** Add your scores for Part A and Part B to determine your total number of correct answers. Turn to the Comprehension Score Graph on page 117. Put an X at the point where the vertical line that represents your lesson intersects your total correct answers, shown along the left-hand side. The right-hand side of the graph will show the percentage of questions you answered correctly.

3. **Complete the Comprehension Skills Profile.** Turn to page 118. Record your incorrect answers for the Part B exercises. The five Part B skills are listed along the bottom. There are five columns of boxes, one column for each question. For every incorrect answer, put an X in a box for that skill.

To get the most benefit from these lessons, you need to take charge of your own progress in improving your reading speed and comprehension. Studying these graphs will help you to see whether your reading rate is increasing and to determine what skills you need to work on. Your teacher will also review the graphs to check your progress.

TO THE TEACHER

About the Series

Timed Readings Plus in Social Studies includes 10 books at reading levels 4–13, with one book at each level. Book One contains material at a fourth-grade reading level; Book Two at a fifth-grade level, and so on. The readability level is determined by the Fry Readability Scale and is not to be confused with grade or age level of the student. The books are designed for use with students at middle school level and above.

The purposes of the series are as follows:

- to provide systematic, structured reading practice that helps students improve their reading rate and comprehension skills

- to give students practice in reading and understanding informational articles in the content area of social studies

- to give students experience in reading various text types—informational, expository, narrative, and prescriptive

- to prepare students for taking standardized tests that include timed reading passages in various content areas

- to provide materials with a wide range of reading levels so that students can continue to practice and improve their reading rate and comprehension skills

Because the books are designed for use with students at designated reading levels rather than in a particular grade, the social studies topics in this series are not correlated to any grade-level curriculum. Most standardized tests require students to read and comprehend social studies passages. This series provides an opportunity for students to become familiar with the particular requirements of reading social studies. For example, the vocabulary in a social studies article is important. Students need to know certain words in order to understand the concepts and the information.

Each book in the series contains 25 two-part lessons. Part A focuses on improving reading rate. This section of the lesson consists of a 400-word timed informational article on a social studies topic followed by two multiple-choice exercises. Recalling Facts includes five fact questions; Understanding Ideas includes five critical thinking questions.

Part B concentrates on building mastery in critical areas of comprehension. This section consists of a nontimed passage—the "plus" passage—followed by five exercises that address five major comprehension skills. The passage varies in length; its subject matter relates to the content of the timed selection.

Timed Reading and Comprehension

Timed reading is the best-known method of improving reading speed. There is no point in someone's reading at an accelerated speed if the person does not understand what she or he is reading. Nothing is more important than comprehension in reading. The main purpose of reading is to gain knowledge and insight, to understand the information that the writer and the text are communicating.

Few students will be able to read a passage once and answer all of the questions correctly. A score of 70 or 80 percent correct is normal. If the student gets 90 or 100 percent correct, he or she is either reading too slowly or the material is at too low a reading level. A comprehension or critical thinking score of less than 70 percent indicates a need for improvement.

One method of improving comprehension and critical thinking skills is for the student to go back and study each incorrect answer. First, the student should reread the question carefully. It is surprising how many students get the wrong answer simply because they have not read the question carefully. Then the student should look back in the passage to find the place where the question is answered, reread that part of the passage, and think about how to arrive at the correct answer. It is important to be able to recognize a correct answer when it is embedded in the text. Teacher guidance or class discussion will help the student find an answer.

Speed Versus Comprehension

It is not unusual for comprehension scores to decline as reading rate increases during the early weeks of timed readings. If this happens, students should attempt to level off their speed—but not lower it—and concentrate more on comprehension. Usually, if students maintain the higher speed and concentrate on comprehension, scores will gradually improve and within a week or two be back up to normal levels of 70 to 80 percent.

It is important to achieve a proper balance between speed and comprehension. An inefficient reader typically reads everything at one speed, usually slowly. Some poor readers, however, read rapidly but without satisfactory comprehension. It is important to achieve a balance between speed and comprehension. The practice that this series provides enables students to increase their reading speed while maintaining normal levels of comprehension.

Getting Started

As a rule, the passages in a book designed to improve reading speed should be relatively easy. The student should not have much difficulty with the vocabulary or the subject matter. Don't worry about the passages being too easy; students should see how quickly and efficiently they can read a passage.

Begin by assigning students to a level. A student should start with a book that is one level below his or her current reading level. If a student's reading level is not known, a suitable starting point would be one or two levels below the student's present grade in school.

Introduce students to the contents and format of the book they are using. Examine the book to see how it is organized. Talk about the parts of each lesson. Discuss the purpose of timed reading and the use of the progress graphs at the back of the book.

Timing the Reading

One suggestion for timing the reading is to have all students begin reading the selection at the same time. After one minute, write on the board the time that has elapsed and begin updating it at 10-second intervals (1:00, 1:10, 1:20, etc.). Another option is to have individual students time themselves with a stopwatch.

Teaching a Lesson

Part A

1. Give students the signal to begin previewing the lesson. Allow 20 seconds, then discuss special terms or vocabulary that students found.

2. Use one of the methods described above to time students as they read the passage. (Include the 20-second preview time as part of the first minute.) Tell students to write down the last time shown on the board or the stopwatch when they finish reading. Have them record the time in the designated space after the passage.

3. Next, have students complete the exercises in Part A. Work with them to check their answers, using the Answer Key that begins on page 114. Have them circle incorrect answers, mark the correct answers, and then record the numbers of correct answers for Part A on the appropriate line at the end of the lesson. Correct responses to eight or more questions indicate satisfactory comprehension and recall.

Part B

1. Have students read the Part B passage and complete the exercises that follow it. Directions are provided with each exercise. Correct responses require deliberation and discrimination.

2. Work with students to check their answers. Then discuss the answers with them and have them record the number of correct answers for Part B at the end of the lesson.

Have students study the correct answers to the questions they answered incorrectly. It is important that they understand why a particular answer is correct or incorrect.

Have them reread relevant parts of a passage to clarify an answer. An effective cooperative activity is to have students work in pairs to discuss their answers, explain why they chose the answers they did, and try to resolve differences.

Monitoring Progress

Have students find their total correct answers for the lesson and record their reading time and scores on the graphs on pages 116 and 117. Then have them complete the Comprehension Skills Profile on page 118. For each incorrect response to a question in Part B, students should mark an X in the box above each question type.

The legend on the Reading Rate graph automatically converts reading times to words-per-minute rates. The Comprehension Score graph automatically converts the raw scores to percentages.

These graphs provide a visual record of a student's progress. This record gives the student and you an opportunity to evaluate the student's progress and to determine the types of exercises and skills he or she needs to concentrate on.

Diagnosis and Evaluation

The following are typical reading rates.

Slow Reader—150 Words Per Minute

Average Reader—250 Words Per Minute

Fast Reader—350 Words Per Minute

A student who consistently reads at an average or above-average rate (with satisfactory comprehension) is ready to advance to the next book in the series.

A column of Xs in the Comprehension Skills Profile indicates a specific comprehension weakness. Using the profile, you can assess trends in student performance and suggest remedial work if necessary.

States of the Middle Atlantic Region

The United States is made up of 50 states divided into five distinct regions. Located on the East Coast, the Middle Atlantic region was one of the earliest to be colonized. European explorers settled in the areas that are the present-day states of New York, New Jersey, Pennsylvania, Delaware, and Maryland. These states have much in common. Each was among the original 13 states that fought for independence and ratified the U.S. Constitution.

Although the Dutch were the first to settle there, Pennsylvania takes its name from William Penn, who founded it in 1681. Penn, an English Quaker, sought to establish a colony to promote freedom and equality. The colony became a commonwealth in 1776. Its largest city, Philadelphia, was the country's first capital. Many momentous events took place there during the Revolution. Among them were the signing of the Declaration of Independence and the drafting and signing of the Constitution.

In 1664 Dutch merchants started the Dutch West India Company with posts along the Hudson River. These posts grew into New Netherland. New Netherland had a thriving river trade and an excellent harbor. New Jersey was initially part of the colony of New Netherland. First colonized by Dutch and Swedish settlers, the state is named for the Isle of Jersey, of which Sir George Carteret, one of its original owners, was governor. The state made many important contributions to the American Revolution. However, it is perhaps best remembered for Washington's crossing of the Delaware River to fight the British at the Battle of Trenton.

New York, also part of New Netherland, was settled by the Dutch in 1624 but was seized by England in 1664 and renamed for the Duke of York. Throughout the Revolution, the British held New York City. New York State was the site of fierce battles. New York City—for a short time—served as the capital of the new nation.

The English explorer Henry Hudson discovered Delaware in 1609, but Swedish, Finnish, and Dutch colonists settled it. It was first a Dutch colony; but it was seized by the English in 1664, recaptured by the Dutch, and then returned to the English.

Charles I of England chartered Maryland in 1632. It was named for his queen consort, Henrietta Maria. Cecilius Calvert, second Baron Baltimore, established the colony as a haven for those fleeing religious persecution. Annapolis was the site of the Treaty of Paris, which ended the Revolutionary War.

Reading Time _____

Recalling Facts

1. The first capital of the United States was located in
   - ❑ a. New York.
   - ❑ b. New Jersey.
   - ❑ c. Pennsylvania.

2. New Jersey was named for the place where _____ had been one of its original owners.
   - ❑ a. William Penn
   - ❑ b. Nathan Jersey
   - ❑ c. Sir George Carteret

3. Which of the following was *not* part of New Netherland?
   - ❑ a. Delaware
   - ❑ b. New York
   - ❑ c. New Jersey

4. Delaware was originally settled by colonists from
   - ❑ a. England, Sweden, and Finland.
   - ❑ b. Sweden, Finland, and the Netherlands.
   - ❑ c. England, Finland, and the Netherlands.

5. The colony of Maryland was established as a haven for those fleeing
   - ❑ a. religious persecution.
   - ❑ b. famine and poverty.
   - ❑ c. imprisonment under English rule.

Understanding Ideas

6. One can conclude that the Dutch
   - ❑ a. were the first arrivals to the United States.
   - ❑ b. played a major role in the colonization of the United States.
   - ❑ c. had little influence in the colonization of the United States.

7. The Middle Atlantic states had
   - ❑ a. the same colonial history.
   - ❑ b. important roles in the American Revolution.
   - ❑ c. little influence in establishing a new government.

8. Holding New York City was
   - ❑ a. more of a symbolic than a strategic victory for the British.
   - ❑ b. insignificant militarily during the American Revolution.
   - ❑ c. critical to the strategies of both England and the United States.

9. The Middle Atlantic region was
   - ❑ a. too divided in its beliefs to have a great impact on the early stages of democracy.
   - ❑ b. instrumental in establishing important early principles of democracy in the United States.
   - ❑ c. led by colonists who remained loyal to England.

10. What is the main idea of the passage?
    - ❑ a. The Middle Atlantic States are New Jersey, New York, Pennsylvania, Maryland, and Delaware.
    - ❑ b. The Middle Atlantic states have much history in common, including their important roles in the founding of the nation.
    - ❑ c. Each region of the United States was settled in a different way.

William Penn's Legacy

William Penn contributed much to the early history of the United States. Although he may be best known as the founder of Pennsylvania, Penn's influence also extended to the other states of the Middle Atlantic region.

As a Quaker in England, Penn was jailed for his beliefs. He thought that the American colonies offered a chance for equal rights and religious freedom. He wanted to start settlements there as a "holy experiment." In 1681 Penn and some others purchased East Jersey. He later received a charter for Pennsylvania. He was also granted land, first annexed to New York, that would later become the state of Delaware.

Many people considered the *Frame of Government of Pennsylvania,* Penn's plan for the colony, a document that was ahead of its time. One of the country's founders, Thomas Jefferson, called Penn "the greatest law-giver the world has produced." Penn was also responsible for planning and naming the city of Philadelphia, which means "the city of brotherly love." In the early days of the colony, he established good relations with the Native Americans of the area. This helped pave the way for the future growth of the colonies.

In addition to his writings on government, Penn wrote expansively on religion and other issues. Today his writings can be found in libraries throughout the country.

1. Recognizing Words in Context

Find the word *expansively* in the passage. One definition below is closest to the meaning of that word. One definition has the opposite or nearly the opposite meaning. The remaining definition has a completely different meaning. Label the definitions C for *closest,* O for *opposite or nearly opposite,* and D for *different.*

_____ a. broadly

_____ b. slowly

_____ c. narrowly

2. Distinguishing Fact from Opinion

Two of the statements below present *facts,* which can be proved. The other statement is an *opinion,* which expresses someone's thoughts or beliefs. Label the statements F for *fact* and O for *opinion.*

_____ a. William Penn sought to escape religious persecution.

_____ b. William Penn was the most important of the early colonists who came to America.

_____ c. William Penn got along well with Native Americans.

3. Keeping Events in Order

Number the statements below 1, 2, and 3 to show the order in which the events took place.

_____ a. Penn planned the city of Philadelphia.

_____ b. Penn suffered religious persecution.

_____ c. Penn came to America.

4. Making Correct Inferences

Two of the statements below are correct *inferences,* or reasonable guesses. They are based on information in the passage. The other statement is an incorrect, or faulty, inference. Label the statements C for *correct* inference and F for *faulty* inference.

_____ a. Penn's belief in the principals of equality and religious freedom can be seen in both his writings and his deeds.

_____ b. Penn's idea of government influenced the political thinking of Thomas Jefferson.

_____ c. All of the colonists of Pennsylvania were Quakers.

5. Understanding Main Ideas

One of the statements below expresses the main idea of the passage. One statement is too general, or too broad. The other explains only part of the passage; it is too narrow. Label the statements M for *main idea,* B for *too broad,* and N for *too narrow.*

_____ a. Many principled people such as William Penn worked to establish the early colonies.

_____ b. William Penn played a key role in the settlement of the Middle Atlantic region.

_____ c. William Penn was a Quaker who was guided by his religious beliefs.

Correct Answers, Part A _____

Correct Answers, Part B _____

Total Correct Answers _____

The Shy Angel

Clara Barton, founder of the American Red Cross, gained worldwide honor for her dedication to easing human suffering. Her tireless work amid the filth, disease, and danger of Civil War battles earned her the nickname "Angel of the Battlefield."

Barton was born into a liberal, freethinking family in 1821. She was much younger than her four brothers and sisters, all of whom happily tutored her in math and reading. As a result, by the time she entered school at the age of three, Barton could read, do simple arithmetic, and spell three-syllable words. She easily kept up with the older children academically but did not fit in with them socially.

Concerned about their daughter's difficulty in making friends, Barton's parents sent her to boarding school. They hoped that it would make her more comfortable with her peers. Unfortunately, it had the opposite effect. Barton lost her appetite and cried constantly. After only one term, she was brought home. From age 11 to 13, Barton stayed out of school to nurse her older brother through a serious injury. She volunteered her time tutoring children and caring for poor families during a smallpox outbreak.

Barton was 40 years old and working in the U.S. Patent Office in Washington, D.C., when the Civil War broke out in 1861. The sight of wounded soldiers touched her deeply. She began to collect and distribute food, bandages, medicines, and other supplies for the Union army. Barton risked her life to transport wagonloads of supplies to the front lines. There, with little concern for her own safety, she cooked meals, assisted surgeons, and comforted wounded soldiers, even as bullets whizzed around her.

Eventually the stress and toil took its toll. Barton collapsed, ill with typhoid fever. When she recovered, her doctors prescribed a long, restful trip to Europe. It was there that she learned of an organization based in Switzerland—called the International Red Cross—whose work mirrored her own.

Shortly after Barton arrived back home in 1873, her sister died, and Barton fell into a deep depression. While recuperating at a health facility in New York, she began planning and lobbying for the establishment of an American wing of the International Red Cross. Although at first the government resisted, Barton's efforts finally paid off. The American Red Cross was officially organized on May 21, 1881. Her influence lives on today in the work of the organization she founded.

Reading Time _____

Recalling Facts

1. Clara Barton founded the
   - ❑ a. U.S. Patent Office.
   - ❑ b. American Red Cross.
   - ❑ c. International Red Cross.

2. As a result of her wartime work, Barton fell ill with
   - ❑ a. depression.
   - ❑ b. typhoid fever.
   - ❑ c. loss of appetite.

3. Barton stayed out of school from the ages of 11 to 13 to
   - ❑ a. travel to Europe.
   - ❑ b. nurse her brother after an accident.
   - ❑ c. care for poor families during a smallpox outbreak.

4. The American Red Cross was founded in
   - ❑ a. 1821.
   - ❑ b. 1861.
   - ❑ c. 1881.

5. During the Civil War, Barton
   - ❑ a. worked in Washington, D.C.
   - ❑ b. assisted doctors and soldiers on the battlefield.
   - ❑ c. lobbied for establishment of the American Red Cross.

Understanding Ideas

6. Which of the following traits best describes Barton?
   - ❑ a. charismatic
   - ❑ b. philanthropic
   - ❑ c. humanitarian

7. Barton nursed soldiers during the Civil War because she
   - ❑ a. wanted the Union army to win.
   - ❑ b. gained satisfaction from easing people's suffering.
   - ❑ c. wanted to prove that starting an American wing of the International Red Cross was good.

8. Barton's ability to work under harsh battlefield conditions probably demonstrates that
   - ❑ a. she had ambitions to be heroic.
   - ❑ b. she did not feel fear.
   - ❑ c. her need to serve others outweighed her concern for her personal safety.

9. Which of the following suggests that Barton felt awkward around her peers?
   - ❑ a. She was unhappy at school.
   - ❑ b. She volunteered her time tutoring young children.
   - ❑ c. It took her several years to convince the U.S. government to support the Red Cross.

10. From the passage, one can infer that
    - ❑ a. Barton's nervous temperament interfered with her work.
    - ❑ b. Barton succeeded because she was not distracted by social activities.
    - ❑ c. Barton's strength, bravery, and compassion enabled her to succeed despite her shyness.

A Woman with a Flare for Success

When her inventor husband died in 1848, Martha Coston, at the age of 21, became a widow with four children to support and little money. Eleven years later, she would patent an invention that would help win the Civil War. Coston's drive and talent placed her among history's most accomplished women.

Shortly after her husband's death, Coston, sorting through papers, found plans for a type of flare that ships could use to communicate with one another at night. In dire need of income, Coston sent samples to the U.S. Navy for testing. The Navy acknowledged that the idea was great. However, it reported that Coston's flares did not work.

Coston refined her husband's design. With no business or science experience, she directed a team of chemists as they devised formulas and conducted experiments. Finally, her design was successful. She patented her red, white, and green "pyrotechnic night signals" in 1859. Two years later, she sold the patent to the Navy but received only $20,000, a fraction of its value.

In 1861 the Civil War broke out. Coston's factory churned out thousands of signal flares but was paid only their cost by the Navy. The flares played an important role in the capture of blockade runners, boats that tried to sneak past Union blockades of Confederate ports.

1. **Recognizing Words in Context**

   Find the word *dire* in the passage. One definition below is closest to the meaning of that word. One definition has the opposite or nearly the opposite meaning. The remaining definition has a completely different meaning. Label the definitions C for *closest*, O for *opposite or nearly opposite*, and D for *different*.

   _____ a. dreadful

   _____ b. delightful

   _____ c. skillful

2. **Distinguishing Fact from Opinion**

   Two of the statements below present *facts*, which can be proved. The other statement is an *opinion*, which expresses someone's thoughts or beliefs. Label the statements F for *fact* and O for *opinion*.

   _____ a. Coston's flares played an important role in the capture of blockade runners.

   _____ b. Coston patented her "pyrotechnic night signals" in 1859.

   _____ c. Coston was the most accomplished woman of her time.

19

3. Keeping Events in Order

Number the statements below 1, 2, and 3 to show the order in which the historical events took place.

_____ a. Coston patented her signal flares.

_____ b. The Civil War broke out.

_____ c. Coston's husband died.

4. Making Correct Inferences

Two of the statements below are correct *inferences*, or reasonable guesses. They are based on information in the passage. The other statement is an incorrect, or faulty, inference. Label the statements C for *correct* inference and F for *faulty* inference.

_____ a. Communication between ships is central to naval wartime victory.

_____ b. Making money was the only reason Coston worked to perfect her signal flares.

_____ c. Coston's dedication and perseverance were key factors in her success.

5. Understanding Main Ideas

One of the statements below expresses the main idea of the passage. One statement is too general, or too broad. The other explains only part of the passage; it is too narrow. Label the statements M for *main idea*, B for *too broad*, and N for *too narrow*.

_____ a. Martha Coston's signal flares were patented as "pyrotechnic night signals."

_____ b. Signal flares are a means of communication.

_____ c. Martha Coston's unique drive and talent led to an invention that contributed to the Union victory in the Civil War.

Correct Answers, Part A _____

Correct Answers, Part B _____

Total Correct Answers _____

Australian Aborigines: Living with a Land and a Legacy

The people known as Australian aborigines were the first human beings on the continent of Australia. (The word *aborigine* means "from the beginning" in Latin.) Arriving at least 40,000 years ago, they occupied most of the continent some 10,000 years later.

The climate was harsh. Sweltering heat and periodic droughts were unfavorable to the growth of crops. Also, there were no native herd animals that could be tamed and used to plow the land. As a result, the aborigines led a nomadic life and did not acquire many possessions. Their tools had to be portable or makeshift (used in one place and then abandoned). One of their tools, the boomerang, is unique among early tools. Although other early hunter-gatherers threw sticks to bring down game, the boomerang's aerodynamic shape ensured that it would return to the thrower if it failed to hit its target.

Another major influence on the aboriginal way of life was the people's mythology. These beliefs spelled out the laws by which they lived and their ideals of harmony and equality. The aborigines believed that their ancestors, mythical beings, created the world and everything in it—land, plants, animals, and people—during "the dreaming." These beings passed along their legacy, known as "the dreamtime," to their descendants. This bequest was made known through the dreams of certain revered old men. The aborigines believed that their purpose in life was to live in agreement with this legacy—in harmony with it, the land, and its inhabitants, rather than in competition with others.

Early aborigines lived in social groups determined by their beliefs and the land itself. Because of the harsh climate and the aborigines' nomadic lifestyle, they lived in small bands rather than large settlements. Their mythology connected them to a certain region of land as well as to the plants and animals found there. This resulted in aborigines' living in "estate groups" that were generally related on the male side. The males in the group were the guardians of the "estate." They engaged in sacred rites and rituals intended to renew and sustain the land and its inhabitants. There was no centralized leadership or government, nor were aborigines divided into social classes. Instead, they relied on their belief in their legacy, and their need to live in agreement with their ancestors' wishes, to ensure that group members lived in accordance with society's rules and in harmony with one another.

Reading Time _____

Recalling Facts

1. The aboriginal boomerang was an early throwing tool, unique in that it
   - ❏ a. could return to the thrower.
   - ❏ b. was capable of bringing down game.
   - ❏ c. was portable and could be carried from one place to another.

2. In aboriginal mythology, the world was created by
   - ❏ a. mythical ancestors.
   - ❏ b. certain revered elderly men.
   - ❏ c. estate groups.

3. According to the passage, an early aboriginal male would most likely become a
   - ❏ a. farmer.
   - ❏ b. hunter.
   - ❏ c. leader.

4. For an aborigine, "dreamtime" is
   - ❏ a. the creation of the world.
   - ❏ b. the legacy passed along to the aborigines from their ancestors.
   - ❏ c. one of the sacred rites and rituals practiced by the guardians of the estate.

5. According to the passage, early aborigines did not domesticate animals because
   - ❏ a. they were nomads.
   - ❏ b. there were no herd animals that they could use as stock.
   - ❏ c. hunting and eating animals was preferred over taming them.

Understanding Ideas

6. Which of the following pairs of adjectives best describes early aborigines?
   - ❏ a. dynamic and warlike
   - ❏ b. imaginative but greedy
   - ❏ c. classless and noncompetitive

7. Two factors primarily responsible for the aborigines' way of life were
   - ❏ a. their sacred rites and rituals.
   - ❏ b. the animals that they hunted and their ancestors.
   - ❏ c. the nature of the land that they lived in and their own mythology.

8. It is likely that a nomadic lifestyle in a harsh climate necessitated living in small bands rather than in large settlements because
   - ❏ a. small bands were more mobile.
   - ❏ b. large settlements were expensive.
   - ❏ c. it was easier to guard the land with smaller bands.

9. From the passage, one can conclude that among early aborigines
   - ❏ a. few people broke social rules.
   - ❏ b. many people deviated from society's expectations.
   - ❏ c. most people were confused about what rules to follow.

10. From the passage, one can conclude that early aborigines
    - ❏ a. spent most of their time developing unique tools.
    - ❏ b. lived in a sacred relationship with their environment.
    - ❏ c. worked hard to develop permanent farming communities.

Early Tools and Toolmaking

In its earliest stages, technology consisted of toolmaking. The Paleolithic period (Old Stone Age) has three subdivisions. Each is defined by changes in human toolmaking.

During the Lower Paleolithic period (150 thousand to 2.5 million years ago), a pebble might be used for pounding, digging, or scraping, or a large stone might be struck against an easily splintered rock, producing sharp-edged flakes for cutting.

An important tool appeared during the Middle Paleolithic period (40 thousand to 150 thousand years ago). It was the symmetrical hand ax. A bone hammer was employed to administer a series of precise strikes that resulted in a carefully chiseled disk. The toolmaker had to be intelligent to create such a tool.

The tools of the Upper Paleolithic period (10 thousand to 40 thousand years ago) were characterized by portability and diversification. Early hunters carried "tool kits." They used the kits to make tools that were suited to a variety of purposes. They made projectiles, scrapers for cleaning hides, borers, and *burins* (engravers) to decorate bone. One very important innovation was the spear thrower, a simple device still in use by Australian aborigines. This weapon extended the human arm's range and force. The extension helped early people to hunt migrating animals successfully.

1. **Recognizing Words in Context**

    Find the word *diversification* in the passage. One definition below is closest to the meaning of that word. One definition has the opposite or nearly the opposite meaning. The remaining definition has a completely different meaning. Label the definitions C for *closest*, O for *opposite or nearly opposite*, and D for *different*.

    _____ a. creative design

    _____ b. ability to be used in a variety of ways

    _____ c. creation for a single purpose

2. **Distinguishing Fact from Opinion**

    Two of the statements below present *facts*, which can be proved. The other statement is an *opinion*, which expresses someone's thoughts or beliefs. Label the statements F for *fact* and O for *opinion*.

    _____ a. The Paleolithic period consists of three subdivisions defined by changes in human toolmaking.

    _____ b. The toolmaker was more intelligent than hunters.

    _____ c. The spear thrower is still in use by Australian aborigines.

3. Keeping Events in Order

Number the statements below 1, 2, and 3 to show the order in which the historical events took place.

_____ a. The spear thrower was first used.

_____ b. The symmetrical hand ax first appeared.

_____ c. The primary tools used were pebbles and flakes from splintered rock.

4. Making Correct Inferences

Two of the statements below are correct *inferences,* or reasonable guesses. They are based on information in the passage. The other statement is an incorrect, or faulty, inference. Label the statements C for *correct* inference and F for *faulty* inference.

_____ a. Different stones have different properties that toolmakers can make use of.

_____ b. Hunters of the Upper Paleolithic period could use their tool kits to repair lost or damaged weapons.

_____ c. Bone is a better material for tools than rock.

5. Understanding Main Ideas

One of the statements below expresses the main idea of the passage. One statement is too general, or too broad. The other explains only part of the passage; it is too narrow. Label the statements M for *main idea,* B for *too broad,* and N for *too narrow.*

_____ a. The Paleolithic period (Old Stone Age) consists of three subdivisions defined by changes in human toolmaking.

_____ b. The tools of the Upper Paleolithic period were characterized by portability and diversification.

_____ c. In its earliest stages, human technology consisted of toolmaking.

Correct Answers, Part A _____

Correct Answers, Part B _____

Total Correct Answers _____

John F. Kennedy: Soft on Civil Rights?

John F. Kennedy took office as president of the United States in 1961. At that time, African Americans' struggle for civil rights was reaching its peak. Kennedy's response to the crisis was mixed. Many historians believe that political concerns made him limit his support of civil rights protections for minorities.

One of Kennedy's campaign promises was to end discrimination in public housing. He would do so, he said, by executive order, "with the stroke of a pen." This promise helped him to win almost three-quarters of the African American vote. After he took office, however, many found his actions in support of civil rights to be less than expected. Kennedy, a Democrat, had only a slight majority in Congress. He believed that by pushing the cause of civil rights, he would lose the support of Southern Democrats. When he still had not signed the promised order after two years, civil rights supporters reminded him of his pledge by sending pens to the White House.

Kennedy planned to introduce civil rights legislation in his second term. By that time, he believed, most of his program would have been passed. However, events in his first term forced him to take direct action. In 1962 an African American student enrolled at the University of Mississippi for the first time in its history. Rioting broke out on campus, and Kennedy sent 3 thousand federal troops to restore order. The following year, Kennedy put the Alabama National Guard under federal authority. The guards were to control the rioting and ensure that African Americans would be allowed to enroll in public universities throughout the state. In a speech shortly after these events, he declared to Congress, "It ought to be possible . . . for every American to enjoy the privileges of being American without regard to his race or his color."

Congress took up the challenge and began debate on a civil rights bill; but when Kennedy was assassinated in November 1963, the bill had not yet been passed. Although Kennedy's successor, Lyndon Baines Johnson, supported it, debate in Congress was heated. Opponents attempted to kill the bill with a 75-day filibuster, a debate designed to cause delay. In 1964, however, Johnson signed the Civil Rights Act into law. The law protects the rights of minorities to vote and have free access to public facilities. The Civil Rights Act of 1964 stands today as one of the strongest U.S. civil rights laws.

Reading Time _____

Recalling Facts

1. John F. Kennedy's civil rights legislation became law in
   ❏ a. 1961.
   ❏ b. 1963.
   ❏ c. 1964.

2. Civil rights supporters sent a message that Kennedy was acting too slowly to end public housing discrimination by
   ❏ a. rioting in Alabama.
   ❏ b. sending him pens in the mail.
   ❏ c. threatening to vote him out of office.

3. Rioting broke out in Mississippi after
   ❏ a. Kennedy was elected president.
   ❏ b. an African American student enrolled at a university there.
   ❏ c. important civil rights legislation was passed in the state of Mississippi.

4. Kennedy responded to unrest in Alabama by
   ❏ a. sending in federal troops.
   ❏ b. signing a civil rights bill into law.
   ❏ c. bringing the state's national guard under federal authority.

5. The Civil Rights Act of 1964 made it no longer legal to
   ❏ a. march in protest against equal rights for African Americans.
   ❏ b. prevent minorities from using certain public facilities.
   ❏ c. try to convince minorities to vote for a particular candidate in an election.

Understanding Ideas

6. Debate on the civil rights bill was probably so heated because
   ❏ a. the American public did not want the bill.
   ❏ b. Kennedy was no longer alive to support the bill.
   ❏ c. lawmakers representing the Southern states opposed the bill.

7. Kennedy may have delayed giving full support to civil rights because he
   ❏ a. believed that the country was not ready for equal rights.
   ❏ b. was concerned about losing the support of Southern Democrats.
   ❏ c. was afraid that passing civil rights laws would cause rioting.

8. Kennedy's promise to end discrimination in public housing probably
   ❏ a. almost cost him the election.
   ❏ b. won him African American votes.
   ❏ c. was easy to accomplish.

9. Kennedy's political approach to civil rights suggests that
   ❏ a. he was more concerned with other parts of his program.
   ❏ b. Democrats opposed civil rights protection for minorities.
   ❏ c. he acted in support of civil rights only to prevent violence.

10. The fact that a bill can be "killed" by filibuster suggests that
    ❏ a. a bill will die if it is not voted on during a particular period.
    ❏ b. lawmakers stage filibusters when a bill has no chance of passing.
    ❏ c. supporters of a bill will change their minds if the debate continues long enough.

Bringing History Back to the White House

Shortly after her husband had been elected president, Jacqueline Kennedy was taken on a visit to the White House. She was aghast. Long fascinated with the history of the presidency, she believed that as an American treasure the White House deserved care and impressive presentation.

The First Lady went to work to restore the public rooms to their original appearance, organizing the White House Fine Arts Committee to carry out the work. She also established the White House Historical Association, which published the first-ever White House guidebook. The committee used profits from the sale of the book to locate historical treasures that were in collections throughout the country.

Mrs. Kennedy always stressed that her work was much more than redecorating. The effort was a work of "scholarship," she said. Returning possessions of presidents such as Washington, Lincoln, and Madison to the White House was one of the committee's greatest successes.

However, Mrs. Kennedy did not stop at restoration. She made the White House a living center of the arts by welcoming leading artists, writers, and entertainers. The White House, she thought, should serve not only as the seat of political power in the United States but also as one of the country's chief cultural centers. The tradition she began 40 years ago continues to this day.

1. **Recognizing Words in Context**

   Find the word *aghast* in the passage. One definition below is closest to the meaning of that word. One definition has the opposite or nearly the opposite meaning. The remaining definition has a completely different meaning. Label the definitions C for *closest*, O for *opposite or nearly opposite*, and D for *different*.

   _____ a. pleased

   _____ b. inspired

   _____ c. dismayed

2. **Distinguishing Fact from Opinion**

   Two of the statements below present *facts*, which can be proved. The other statement is an *opinion*, which expresses someone's thoughts or beliefs. Label the statements F for *fact* and O for *opinion*.

   _____ a. Mrs. Kennedy was shocked by the condition of the White House.

   _____ b. The Fine Arts Committee found many historically important items.

   _____ c. The White House restoration seems more important than it really was.

3. Keeping Events in Order

Number the statements below 1, 2, and 3 to show the order in which the events took place.

_____ a. Mrs. Kennedy set up the White House Fine Arts Committee to carry out the restoration work.

_____ b. Mrs. Kennedy visited the White House.

_____ c. Mrs. Kennedy invited cultural figures to appear at the White House.

4. Making Correct Inferences

Two of the statements below are correct *inferences,* or reasonable guesses. They are based on information in the passage. The other statement is an incorrect, or faulty, inference. Label the statements C for *correct* inference and F for *faulty* inference.

_____ a. No one cared about the condition of the White House before Jacqueline Kennedy became First Lady.

_____ b. Mrs. Kennedy worked to restore the White House because she considered the place an important part of American history.

_____ c. Mrs. Kennedy wanted to make the White House a place that Americans would want to visit.

5. Understanding Main Ideas

One of the statements below expresses the main idea of the passage. One statement is too general, or too broad. The other explains only part of the passage; it is too narrow. Label the statements M for *main idea,* B for *too broad,* and N for *too narrow.*

_____ a. The White House is an important American historical site.

_____ b. Jacqueline Kennedy's restoration of the White House made it a place of beauty suited to its historical significance.

_____ c. The restoration work required that historical presidential items be located and brought back to the White House.

Correct Answers, Part A _____

Correct Answers, Part B _____

Total Correct Answers _____

Film and the Depression

In October 1929, the U.S. stock market crashed, ushering in the Great Depression. At that time, film as a form of entertainment was fairly new. The first "talkie," or movie with sound, *The Jazz Singer,* had been released two years earlier. Like any young industry, film was undergoing changes. These changes became more pronounced as filmmakers reflected the tastes and concerns of their viewers.

The Depression filled Americans with despair and shattered their trust in the social system. Bread lines and soup kitchens fed hungry citizens. Desperate workers struggled to earn pennies by hawking apples on the streets. The films of the early 1930s reflected these harsh realities. Exploitation, a common theme, was portrayed in romantic relationships, work, and law. Characters used immoral and ruthless means to get the better of one another. Stock roles included the fallen woman, the forgotten man, the abandoned youth, the greedy capitalist, and oppressed workers. Topics related to social chaos and the evils of class inequity were the norm in dramas and comedies. Gangster films, in which "bad guys" not only starred but also often came out on top, were among the most popular films of the early 1930s.

People seemed to enjoy this steely view of life. But some groups saw this trend as dangerous. In 1933 the Roman Catholic Church's Legion of Decency threatened to organize boycotts of any film it judged to be immoral. Hollywood responded by setting up a production code in 1934. Films began to tell stories of wholesomeness. Law officers, such as the Western sheriff, replaced gangsters as heroes. Wealth was no longer an evil but a supreme good.

This mood shift spawned a new genre of film—the screwball comedy. Sexuality was now expressed through clever wordplay as men and women revealed their attraction for one another in comic battles. The rich were no longer portrayed as exploiting the poor. Now they were carefree and wacky; and if they made mistakes that hurt those less fortunate, it was not from greed but from ignorance. Happy endings, in which such characters saw the error of their ways and were rewarded with true love, money, or both, were essential to the formula. What films lost in dealing frankly with the more troubling side of life they gained in a new set of fresh, amusing ways to offer hope that the American dream really was within reach of every American.

Reading Time _____

Recalling Facts

1. The first movie with sound was released in
   - ❑ a. 1927.
   - ❑ b. 1929.
   - ❑ c. 1934.

2. The beginning of the Great Depression was sparked by the
   - ❑ a. stock market crash.
   - ❑ b. collapse of the movie industry.
   - ❑ c. formation of bread lines and soup kitchens.

3. Gangster films of the early 1930s portrayed criminals as
   - ❑ a. heroes.
   - ❑ b. forgotten men.
   - ❑ c. evildoers who were punished for their crimes.

4. The actions of groups such as the Roman Catholic Church's Legion of Decency forced the film industry to
   - ❑ a. close many movie houses.
   - ❑ b. portray rich people as corrupt.
   - ❑ c. set up and follow a production code.

5. A movie that features wacky characters who find love, fortune, or both at the film's end is called
   - ❑ a. a carefree comedy.
   - ❑ b. an oddball comedy.
   - ❑ c. a screwball comedy.

Understanding Ideas

6. One thing movies offered Americans in the early 1930s was
   - ❑ a. opportunities to improve their financial status.
   - ❑ b. reassurance that they were not alone in their despair.
   - ❑ c. hope that good people with good intentions would be rewarded in the end.

7. The popularity of the gritty films of the early 1930s suggests that
   - ❑ a. Hollywood was out of touch with what audiences wanted.
   - ❑ b. people like films that reflect their lives, even unpleasant ones.
   - ❑ c. a production code was needed to control what was put in films.

8. Hollywood set up and followed a production code because
   - ❑ a. they did not want to lose audiences.
   - ❑ b. the Depression was easing.
   - ❑ c. producers and directors agreed that their films were immoral.

9. The main difference between the films of the first half of the 1930s and those of the second half is that
   - ❑ a. comedies replaced musicals.
   - ❑ b. crime stories were not made.
   - ❑ c. wholesomeness replaced gritty realism.

10. The development of the screwball comedy is an example of the saying
    - ❑ a. "Necessity is the mother of invention."
    - ❑ b. "Discretion is the better part of valor."
    - ❑ c. "Beauty is in the eye of the beholder."

5 B   Edison's Kinetoscope and the Birth of the Movies

Thomas Alva Edison demonstrated his kinetoscope in 1893. The device was both a camera and a viewer. It looked like a small cabinet with a viewing lens mounted on top. The film ran horizontally past the lens. This device made Edison a pioneer in the motion-picture industry. Later it became one of the world's most popular forms of entertainment.

In 1893 Edison opened a studio in West Orange, New Jersey. There, a team produced the world's first movies. These short films included actualities, advertisements, dramas and comedies, tricks, and reenactments. Kinetoscope parlors soon sprouted up in cities and began to show these films.

The first films were actualities, nonfiction snippets that provided glimpses of famous people, places, and events. The first actualities showed boxers, dancers, clowns, and other performers. After a portable camera was developed, the studio produced films of city and nature scenes, train travel, and news events. One of the most renowned showed the 1897 swearing in of President William McKinley. Another showed the "burial" of the battleship U.S.S. *Maine*, sunk in the Spanish-American War.

Starting in 1913, Edison began to work on a device called a kinetophone that could match sound to films. However, he never perfected the kinetophone. It was abandoned two years later. Soon Edison dropped out of the film industry

1. **Recognizing Words in Context**

Find the word *renowned* in the passage. One definition below is closest to the meaning of that word. One definition has the opposite or nearly the opposite meaning. The remaining definition has a completely different meaning. Label the definitions C for *closest*, O for *opposite or nearly opposite*, and D for *different*.

_____ a. lighthearted

_____ b. discovered

_____ c. famous

2. **Distinguishing Fact from Opinion**

Two of the statements below present *facts*, which can be proved. The other statement is an *opinion*, which expresses someone's thoughts or beliefs. Label the statements F for *fact* and O for *opinion*.

_____ a. Films shot outdoors were superior to those made at Edison's studio.

_____ b. The kinetoscope looked like a small cabinet.

_____ c. Edison's motion-picture complex was large.

3. Keeping Events in Order

Number the statements below 1, 2, and 3 to show the order in which the events took place.

_____ a. Edison began work on a kinetophone.

_____ b. The first public demonstration of Edison's kinetoscope took place.

_____ c. President William McKinley was inaugurated.

4. Making Correct Inferences

Two of the statements below are correct *inferences,* or reasonable guesses. They are based on information in the passage. The other statement is an incorrect, or faulty, inference. Label the statements C for *correct* inference and F for *faulty* inference.

_____ a. Even in the early days of the motion-picture industry, audiences had a variety of films to choose from.

_____ b. Movies using sound technology "caught on" sometime after 1915.

_____ c. Edison dropped out of the motion-picture industry because he was unsuccessful in it.

5. Understanding Main Ideas

One of the statements below expresses the main idea of the passage. One statement is too general, or too broad. The other explains only part of the passage; it is too narrow. Label the statements M for *main idea,* B for *too broad,* and N for *too narrow.*

_____ a. The kinetoscope was one of Thomas Edison's important inventions.

_____ b. Thomas Edison was one of the pioneers of motion-picture technology.

_____ c. Thomas Edison was both a famous inventor and a scientist.

Correct Answers, Part A _____

Correct Answers, Part B _____

Total Correct Answers _____

The Genius of Ancient Rome

In the sixth century B.C., Rome was a minor town in central Italy. Only a few centuries later, it was a bustling city at the center of one of the most powerful empires in history. In its prime, Rome commanded an empire that ringed the Mediterranean. The Roman Empire included England, much of Europe, most of Asia west of the Euphrates River, northern Africa, and all of the islands in between. Why did Rome emerge as one of the greatest powers of all times? There are several related reasons.

To forge an empire, a nation needs vast armies that can fight on numerous fronts. Unlike its neighbors, Rome made it a practice to grant citizenship to any non-Romans joining their cause. They also let all citizens share in the spoils of victory. Such an open-door policy created a steady flow of enlistees who had a stake in the outcome of battle. In addition, the Romans developed an open formation of small groups of soldiers, which had two great advantages. Troops could quickly be mobilized and deployed as needed. Substitutions of fresh soldiers could readily be made for dead or wounded ones.

Once a region came under Roman control, it could go about its business under the authority of a provincial governor. The Romans found it efficient to have their empire administered at the local level, rather than concentrating power in Rome. This was not the case with their legal system, however. The Romans unified a jumble of ancient laws and practices into a coherent whole. No longer was the law subject to a variety of interpretations depending upon who was judging and who was being judged. Rather, the law was predictable and was applied in the same way throughout the empire. The Roman system of governance created stability and produced, through heavy taxation, a steady stream of riches to Rome.

In order to maintain the empire's infrastructure, the ancient Romans focused on building useful structures. They built bridges, huge warehouses, and aqueducts that carried water to the public. They also built apartment buildings, public baths, sewers, and paved roads on which goods or armies could be transported. The Romans' creation of cement was important to their architecture. This substance proved to be far stronger than other building materials of the time.

If the ancient Greeks were brilliant creators and visionary idealists, the ancient Romans were expert technicians and tacticians. They were, in a word, practical.

Reading Time _____

Recalling Facts

1. According to the passage, the genius of the ancient Romans was their
   - ❑ a. idealism.
   - ❑ b. practicality.
   - ❑ c. lack of structure.

2. In the Roman legal system, laws were
   - ❑ a. different in different regions.
   - ❑ b. the same throughout the empire.
   - ❑ c. created by the provincial governors.

3. The Romans preferred cement over other building materials because cement was
   - ❑ a. stronger.
   - ❑ b. more flexible.
   - ❑ c. less expensive.

4. The most important reason that Rome was able to maintain huge armies was that it
   - ❑ a. built roads to move troops.
   - ❑ b. granted foreigners citizenship and a share in the spoils of war.
   - ❑ c. used an open formation of small groups for quick deployment.

5. Controlling an empire made Rome wealthy because
   - ❑ a. the empire ringed the Mediterranean.
   - ❑ b. everyone shared in the spoils of war.
   - ❑ c. the Romans taxed the provinces heavily.

Understanding Ideas

6. In contrast to its legal system, the government within the Roman Empire
   - ❑ a. was stable.
   - ❑ b. varied from locality to locality.
   - ❑ c. was democratic.

7. The success of the Roman Empire was *not* a result of
   - ❑ a. the growth of the city of Rome.
   - ❑ b. Rome's military policies, which guaranteed huge armies.
   - ❑ c. Rome's administrative policies, which kept the empire running smoothly.

8. Which of the following statements best describes the main idea of the passage?
   - ❑ a. The ancient Romans created an empire that lasted for centuries.
   - ❑ b. The ancient Greeks were brilliant inventors and visionary idealists.
   - ❑ c. Rome emerged as one of the greatest imperial powers through its practical approach to society and government.

9. The Romans were exceptionally good at activities related to
   - ❑ a. theater.
   - ❑ b. philosophy.
   - ❑ c. engineering.

10. One can conclude from the passage that the author admires
    - ❑ a. both the ancient Romans and the ancient Greeks.
    - ❑ b. the ancient Greeks more than the ancient Romans.
    - ❑ c. the ancient Romans more than the ancient Greeks.

Augustus and the Pax Romana

In 45 B.C., Roman emperor Julius Caesar adopted his 18-year-old great-nephew Octavian as his son and heir. One year later, the young man was fatherless. Caesar's enemies had murdered him. In the years after Caesar's death, Octavian, Marc Antony (Caesar's second in command), and a man named Lepidus ruled. Gaining poise and military strength, Octavian wrested control first from Lepidus (32 B.C.) and then from Antony (31 B.C.).

Luckily for Rome, Octavian did not plan to build a military dictatorship. Instead, Caesar's heir proved more than equal to the task of governing. He restored order to Rome, dismantled his army, and called for regular elections. Predictably, he was elected consul. He offered to give up his powers, but the Roman Senate rejected his offer. Instead, they bestowed honors upon him. Among them was the title of Augustus, meaning "honored." He soon became known by this name.

Augustus took a Rome that had been in disarray and rebuilt its government, its traditions, and its architecture. Under his rule, the empire expanded and united. The Mediterranean world entered a period of harmony and wealth that became known as the *Pax Romana* (Latin for "Roman peace"). This period lasted for more than 200 years. Augustus died in A.D. 14. Many considered him one of the great administrative geniuses of history.

1. **Recognizing Words in Context**

   Find the word *wrested* in the passage. One definition below is closest to the meaning of that word. One definition has the opposite or nearly the opposite meaning. The remaining definition has a completely different meaning. Label the definitions C for *closest*, O for *opposite or nearly opposite*, and D for *different*.

   _____ a. took by force

   _____ b. gave freely

   _____ c. eased slowly

2. **Distinguishing Fact from Opinion**

   Two of the statements below present *facts*, which can be proved. The other statement is an *opinion*, which expresses someone's thoughts or beliefs. Label the statements F for *fact* and O for *opinion*.

   _____ a. The *Pax Romana* was a period of tranquility and prosperity.

   _____ b. The Senate bestowed upon Octavian the title Augustus, meaning "honored."

   _____ c. Augustus was one of the great administrative geniuses in history.

3. Keeping Events in Order

Number the statements below 1, 2, and 3 to show the order in which the historical events took place.

_____ a. Octavian is elected consul.

_____ b. Octavian, Antony, and Lepidus rule Rome.

_____ c. Julius Caesar is assassinated.

4. Making Correct Inferences

Two of the statements below are correct *inferences,* or reasonable guesses. They are based on information in the passage. The other statement is an incorrect, or faulty, inference. Label the statements C for *correct* inference and F for *faulty* inference.

_____ a. The Roman senators welcomed Octavian's rule.

_____ b. Octavian was not a very good military leader.

_____ c. Octavian was not greedy for personal power.

5. Understanding Main Ideas

One of the statements below expresses the main idea of the passage. One statement is too general, or too broad. The other explains only part of the passage; it is too narrow. Label the statements M for *main idea*, B for *too broad*, and N for *too narrow*.

_____ a. The *Pax Romana* was a period of tranquility and prosperity.

_____ b. Caesar's heir proved more than equal to the task of governing and restored order to the Roman Empire.

_____ c. Fortunately for Rome, Octavian had no desire to establish a military dictatorship.

Correct Answers, Part A _____

Correct Answers, Part B _____

Total Correct Answers _____

Haves and Have-Nots in the 1950s

Many Americans think of the 1950s as a time of poodle skirts, sock hops, two-car garages, soda fountains, tidy suburbs, and wholesome values. With good jobs and money in the bank, many people enjoyed a good lifestyle. But these images make up only part of the 1950s scene. The other side of the landscape was not quite so attractive.

During the decade, the country's gross national product grew by 51 percent. This bull economy was fueled by several factors, including defense spending. Fears of nuclear devastation and global communist takeovers propelled the Cold War, and the Cold War propelled defense spending. Under President Dwight D. Eisenhower, the U.S. government pumped about $350 billion into defense.

Automation—the development of machines to do jobs once done by hand—changed the workforce. Also, many soldiers returning from World War II took advantage of the GI bill. This was a special government program to pay for college tuition. Returning soldiers were eager to fill the growing number of white-collar jobs. Automation did away with many blue-collar jobs, but wages for factory workers rose by 50 percent.

These workers, both blue collar and white collar, joined the middle class. They married and had many children, setting the 18-year period of high birth rates after World War II, known as the baby boom, into motion. Adults were glad that the hardships of the Great Depression and the war years were over. Their children, many of whom had never experienced going without whatever they needed, shared their hunger for consumer goods.

But America had a troubling secret—poverty. Political activist Michael Harrington brought this fact to light in his 1962 book, *The Other America*. Harrington estimated that 50 million Americans lived in poverty. Most people never saw these "other Americans," but anyone who ventured away from the grassy suburbs and shiny downtown areas did. These "other Americans" were hidden away in backwoods hamlets and urban ghettoes. While most Americans were concerned with what to buy next, the underclass lacked proper nutrition, health care, and decent housing. Unnoticed and lacking a political voice, the poor were all but invisible.

These dismal truths inspired President John F. Kennedy to assemble a task force on poverty. After Kennedy's death in 1963, his successor, Lyndon B. Johnson, took up the fight. He launched his "war on poverty," which became one of the chief hallmarks of his presidency.

Reading Time _____

Recalling Facts

1. The president who led the country during the 1950s was
   - ❑ a. Lyndon B. Johnson.
   - ❑ b. John F. Kennedy.
   - ❑ c. Dwight D. Eisenhower.

2. During the 1950s, the gross national product
   - ❑ a. doubled.
   - ❑ b. increased by more than 50 percent.
   - ❑ c. increased by more than $350 billion.

3. A hallmark of the Johnson presidency was
   - ❑ a. World War II.
   - ❑ b. the baby boom.
   - ❑ c. the "war on poverty."

4. Many Americans were unaware of the full extent of poverty in America because
   - ❑ a. there were only 50 million poor people.
   - ❑ b. most poor people lived in out-of-the-way places.
   - ❑ c. the government kept the existence of the poor a secret.

5. The book on poverty that influenced Kennedy was called
   - ❑ a. *The Other America*.
   - ❑ b. *The Silent America*.
   - ❑ c. *The Invisible America*.

Understanding Ideas

6. The baby boom contributed to economic growth in the 1950s by
   - ❑ a. causing the urban population to grow.
   - ❑ b. adding to the population of consumers.
   - ❑ c. increasing the number of white-collar workers.

7. According to the passage, the experience of hardship during the Great Depression and the war years
   - ❑ a. led to the baby boom.
   - ❑ b. made older people afraid to spend money.
   - ❑ c. increased demand for consumer goods in the 1950s.

8. The expression *bull economy* refers to an economy that is
   - ❑ a. weak.
   - ❑ b. strong.
   - ❑ c. uneven.

9. According to the passage, soda fountains, sock hops, and tidy suburbs paint a picture of life in the 1950s that is
   - ❑ a. incomplete.
   - ❑ b. completely false.
   - ❑ c. shallow and meaningless.

10. Automation led to a decrease in the number of
    - ❑ a. white-collar jobs.
    - ❑ b. blue-collar jobs.
    - ❑ c. opportunities for soldiers returning from the war.

Homelessness in the Twenty-first Century

In 2000 the United States economy dipped into economic recession. This caused discomfort and hardship in every level of society; but for many of the nation's poor, discomfort and hardship turned to misery.

A surge in homelessness is probably the most tragic result of a nation's financial woes. In 2002 it was estimated that more than 3 million Americans were homeless because of a lack of affordable housing. Experts suggest that a family should spend no more than 30 percent of its income on housing. In contrast, in some families housing costs gobble up 50 percent or more. An unexpected event, such as missed work or illness, can quickly plunge a family into homelessness.

A January 2003 article in *Time* magazine tells the story of one such family. Until August of 2002, the young couple and their three children rented a two-bedroom apartment for about $350 a month. They barely squeaked by on the husband's $920-a-month take-home pay; so when their rent was raised to $500 a month, they could no longer make ends meet. They were lucky enough to find a three-bedroom shelter provided by Catholic Social Services. Although they admit the shelter is the nicest place they have ever lived, they still long for the time when they again can afford a place of their own.

1. Recognizing Words in Context

Find the word *recession* in the passage. One definition below is closest to the meaning of that word. One definition has the opposite or nearly the opposite meaning. The remaining definition has a completely different meaning. Label the definitions C for *closest*, O for *opposite or nearly opposite*, and D for *different*.

_____ a. change

_____ b. progress

_____ c. decline

2. Distinguishing Fact from Opinion

Two of the statements below present *facts*, which can be proved. The other statement is an *opinion*, which expresses someone's thoughts or beliefs. Label the statements F for *fact* and O for *opinion*.

_____ a. If a family saves money for unexpected expenses, it will never be homeless.

_____ b. Experts suggest that a family should spend no more than 30 percent of its income on housing.

_____ c. One cause of homelessness is lack of affordable housing.

3. Keeping Events in Order

Number the statements below 1, 2, and 3 to show the order in which the events took place.

_____ a. The family's rent was raised to $500 a month.

_____ b. The family was forced to move into a shelter.

_____ c. The family squeaked by on earnings of $920 a month.

4. Making Correct Inferences

Two of the statements below are correct *inferences,* or reasonable guesses. They are based on information in the passage. The other statement is an incorrect, or faulty, inference. Label the statements C for *correct* inference and F for *faulty* inference.

_____ a. Shelters provide a permanent solution to homelessness.

_____ b. Low wages and expensive housing contribute to homelessness.

_____ c. An abundance of low-cost housing might lessen the number of homeless people.

5. Understanding Main Ideas

One of the statements below expresses the main idea of the passage. One statement is too general, or too broad. The other explains only part of the passage; it is too narrow. Label the statements M for *main idea,* B for *too broad,* and N for *too narrow.*

_____ a. In 2002 more than 3 million Americans were homeless.

_____ b. Homelessness has many causes, and the problem is made worse during economic recession.

_____ c. Economic recessions have occurred throughout history.

Correct Answers, Part A _____

Correct Answers, Part B _____

Total Correct Answers _____

I Do, I Do—in Any Tradition

Each religion has distinctive marriage rituals that honor the special relationship between a husband and a wife. Consider the different practices typical of Hinduism, Judaism, and Christianity—for example, the Greek Orthodox Church.

Hinduism is an ancient religion that developed in southern Asia about 4 thousand years ago. Judaism evolved in the Near East over the course of several centuries, ending about twenty-four hundred years ago, during the fifth century B.C. In the Greek Orthodox Church, which originated in Greece, a set of practices called the Byzantine rite is observed.

A traditional Hindu wedding takes place over several days and involves some social activities as well as many religious ones. A Hindu wedding may begin with an exchange of gifts of gold (often rings) and flower garlands. In this way, the groom and the bride welcome each other into their joint life. During the marriage ceremony, which takes place before a sacred fire, the corner of the bride's sari, or dress, is often knotted to a scarf worn by the groom. The couple's right hands are also tied together with a thread that has been blessed. These actions symbolize their union. In the *mangal sutra* ceremony, the groom ties the *thali,* a caste symbol, around the bride's throat, recognizing her as part of his family.

In a Jewish wedding, the bride and groom stand under a *chuppah,* a little canopy that symbolizes the life they will build together. During the course of the ceremony, the bride and groom sip from a glass of wine—a symbol of life and a metaphor for marriage—that has been blessed. Wine starts as grape juice and eventually changes into a drink that represents joy. At the end of the service, after the couple drinks the last drops of wine, the groom crushes the empty wineglass under his heel.

The Greek Orthodox couple does not exchange vows; the actions of the bride and groom are enough to show their willingness to be married. The ceremony has two parts: a betrothal service, when rings are exchanged, and the marriage ritual itself, during which the bride and groom are crowned with wedding crowns. These crowns are emblems that signify that the couple will preside as king and queen in the realm of their home. Toward the end of the ceremony, the couple walks around in a little circle, taking their first steps together as husband and wife.

Reading Time _____

Recalling Facts

1. A traditional Hindu wedding
   - ❏ a. follows the Byzantine rite.
   - ❏ b. often takes place over several days.
   - ❏ c. ends with an exchange of flower garlands.

2. In a Jewish wedding, the *chuppah* is a
   - ❏ a. sacred fire.
   - ❏ b. blessing offered over the wine.
   - ❏ c. symbol of the life the bride and groom will build together.

3. A Greek Orthodox bride and groom
   - ❏ a. do not exchange vows during the ceremony.
   - ❏ b. have their hands tied together during the ceremony.
   - ❏ c. exchange rings after they are crowned with the wedding crowns.

4. A Hindu bride's sari is knotted to her groom's scarf
   - ❏ a. when neither of them is looking.
   - ❏ b. while the priest reads from the Torah.
   - ❏ c. to symbolize their union in marriage.

5. The Greek Orthodox wedding ceremony is divided into two distinct parts, which are
   - ❏ a. the betrothal and the marriage ritual.
   - ❏ b. social and religious activities.
   - ❏ c. the exchange of gifts (often gold rings) and of flower garlands.

Understanding Ideas

6. Marriage is compared with wine in the Jewish ceremony because
   - ❏ a. grapes are harvested in the fall.
   - ❏ b. weddings are mostly a social activity.
   - ❏ c. both are created over time and as a result of changes.

7. In most religions, marriage is
   - ❏ a. generally a brief and casual event.
   - ❏ b. an extremely important ritual in a person's life.
   - ❏ c. primarily an opportunity for friends and families to get together.

8. Of the three religions discussed in this passage, _____ is the most ancient.
   - ❏ a. Judaism
   - ❏ b. Hinduism
   - ❏ c. Christianity

9. One can infer from this passage that a betrothal is most similar to
   - ❏ a. a reception.
   - ❏ b. a wedding vow.
   - ❏ c. an engagement.

10. Which of the following sentences best expresses the main idea of this passage?
    - ❏ a. No two religions interpret marriage the same way.
    - ❏ b. A husband and wife should be king and queen in their home.
    - ❏ c. Most wedding ceremonies focus on the relationship between a husband and wife.

Finding a spouse is a serious matter in most cultures. For Jewish people, this process is called a *shidduch,* or matchmaking. A good match brings together young people whose characters and talents complement each other. It also unites families that share many values.

During the thirteenth and fourteenth centuries, wars and religious persecution broke up well-established Jewish communities and sent many families in search of new homes. It also became harder to make a shidduch for a son or daughter. During this time, the role of the *shadchan,* or matchmaker, evolved from that of respected advisor to paid professional.

The shadchanim traveled throughout Europe. They became very familiar with countless families, learned the details of their histories, and found out what made each one special. Such journeys were not without dangers, however. Robbers lurked along the way, and roads were often in poor repair.

Jewish law recognized that the shadchanim put their lives at risk while performing a unique service. When the bride or groom came from far away, the parents often had to pay the matchmaker a high fee. By the fifteenth century, there were clear guidelines about when, and how much, the shadchan should be paid. There were also other rules concerning unhappy matches as well as extremely successful ones.

1. **Recognizing Words in Context**

   Find the word *match* in the passage. One definition below is closest to the meaning of that word. One definition has the opposite or nearly the opposite meaning. The remaining definition has a completely different meaning. Label the definitions C for *closest,* O for *opposite or nearly opposite,* and D for *different.*

   _____ a. union

   _____ b. breakup

   _____ c. confusion

2. **Distinguishing Fact from Opinion**

   Two of the statements below present *facts,* which can be proved. The other statement is an *opinion,* which expresses someone's thoughts or beliefs. Label the statements F for *fact* and O for *opinion.*

   _____ a. *Shadchan* is the term used by Jewish people for a matchmaker.

   _____ b. Matchmakers traveled from city to city throughout Europe.

   _____ c. A good shidduch is important to all Jewish families.

43

3. Keeping Events in Order

Number the statements below 1, 2, and 3 to show the order in which the events took place.

_____ a. Clear guidelines were established to regulate when, and how much, the shadchan should be paid.

_____ b. Religious persecution broke up many well-established Jewish communities.

_____ c. The shadchan became a paid matchmaker, working for parents who wanted to make a shidduch for a son or daughter.

4. Making Correct Inferences

Two of the statements below are correct *inferences,* or reasonable guesses. They are based on information in the passage. The other statement is an incorrect, or faulty, inference. Label the statements C for *correct* inference and F for *faulty* inference.

_____ a. *Shadchanim* is the plural form of *shadchan.*

_____ b. It was common in the Middle Ages for Jewish parents to choose husbands and wives for their children.

_____ c. Jewish people could not get married without the help of a shadchan.

5. Understanding Main Ideas

One of the statements below expresses the main idea of the passage. One statement is too general, or too broad. The other explains only part of the passage; it is too narrow. Label the statements M for *main idea,* B for *too broad,* and N for *too narrow.*

_____ a. The shadchan, or matchmaker, has played a key role in Jewish society and culture.

_____ b. Matchmakers find mates for people who wish to marry.

_____ c. In the Middle Ages, the work of the shadchanim often put them in danger.

Correct Answers, Part A _____

Correct Answers, Part B _____

Total Correct Answers _____

The Changing Roles of American Women

Women's rights movements first began to emerge in the early 1800s. The Industrial Revolution was changing patterns of work and family life. The rural lifestyle, in which each family produced its own food and household goods, was fading. Freed from the need to labor at home, many middle-class women directed their energies toward social and religious activism.

Some women grew troubled by what they saw as their inferior social status. Some formed movements in support of property and voting rights for women and better education for girls. Their efforts improved women's social and legal standing somewhat. However, women who wanted to excel in the "man's world" faced an uphill battle. They usually had to start with family advantages or conquer huge obstacles.

Elizabeth Blackwell was the first woman to earn a degree as a medical doctor. The only school that would admit her did so as a fluke. The faculty at Geneva Medical College in New York turned the decision over to the all-male student body. Treating the request as a joke, they voted to admit her. When she arrived, townspeople gawked at her. Her male classmates giggled and blushed during certain sensitive anatomy demonstrations. Even so, she graduated first in her class in 1849 and went on to have a long career in medicine.

Maria Mitchell, the first American to discover a comet, had strong support from her father, a Quaker. He believed that girls should have the same education as boys. He observed stars for the U.S. Coast Guard and trained Maria in astronomy. She became famous after her comet discovery. She was voted the first woman member of the American Academy of Arts and Sciences in 1848 and of the Association for the Advancement of Sciences in 1850. In 1865 she became professor of astronomy at Vassar College in New York.

Mary Ann Shadd Cary also had a supportive father. She was born into a free African American family in Delaware in 1823. Her father sent her to a Quaker boarding school in Pennsylvania. At that time, education was not open to African Americans in Delaware. Cary went on to become a teacher, newspaper publisher, and activist. She published the *Provincial Freeman,* using her initials on the masthead instead of her first name to disguise the fact that she was a woman. At the age of 60, she became one of the first American women to earn a law degree.

Reading Time _____

Recalling Facts

1. Traditional rural life began to fade after the start of
   - ❏ a. women's movements.
   - ❏ b. the Industrial Revolution.
   - ❏ c. the Association for the Advancement of Science.

2. Elizabeth Blackwell was the first female
   - ❏ a. doctor.
   - ❏ b. lawyer.
   - ❏ c. astronomer.

3. Maria Mitchell gained fame for her
   - ❏ a. writings on equality.
   - ❏ b. discovery of a comet.
   - ❏ c. work to support the rights of women.

4. Maria Mitchell became a professor at
   - ❏ a. Vassar College.
   - ❏ b. Geneva Medical College.
   - ❏ c. the U.S. Coast Guard Academy.

5. The *Provincial Freeman* was published by
   - ❏ a. Maria Mitchell.
   - ❏ b. Elizabeth Blackwell.
   - ❏ c. Mary Ann Shadd Cary.

Understanding Ideas

6. The Industrial Revolution probably led many people to
   - ❏ a. experience poverty.
   - ❏ b. work at jobs outside the home.
   - ❏ c. move from cities to rural areas.

7. Mary Ann Shadd Cary probably used her initials in her newspaper because
   - ❏ a. the newspaper was aimed at male readers.
   - ❏ b. her name was too long to fit on the masthead.
   - ❏ c. people would not have taken seriously a newspaper published by a woman.

8. During the Industrial Revolution, changes in patterns of work and family life led to changes in
   - ❏ a. people's religious beliefs.
   - ❏ b. the ways that women viewed their roles in life in relation to men's roles.
   - ❏ c. the way in which scientists approached research and scientific thinking.

9. The passage supports the inference that Quakers believed in
   - ❏ a. the need for women doctors.
   - ❏ b. equal educational opportunities for all children.
   - ❏ c. the importance of technology to make household work easier.

10. Maria Mitchell had less difficulty being accepted in her field than other women probably because she
    - ❏ a. did not enter an all-male field.
    - ❏ b. hid the fact that she was a woman.
    - ❏ c. made a scientific discovery for which she became famous.

Helen Keller's Activism

Helen Keller, beloved author and humanitarian, is best known, perhaps, for the story of her extraordinary childhood. Left blind and deaf after an illness at the age of 19 months, she became, as she described it, "a wild, unruly child." When Keller was six years old, however, her parents hired Anne Sullivan to be her teacher. By teaching Keller to communicate with sign language, Sullivan helped Keller escape from her dark, silent, isolated world.

By the time Keller graduated from Radcliffe College, she had become a social activist. She spoke out for the rights of women, workers, and minorities. She supported strikers and campaigned for women's right to vote. In 1909 she joined the Socialist Party and worked on behalf of such socialist causes as trade unions. Keller also worked to put an end to child labor. As a pacifist, she spoke out against U.S. involvement in World War I.

In the course of her work, Keller learned that blindness most often struck the poor because it was often caused by work accidents and hazardous living conditions. She decided that her life's work was to be a spokesperson for the blind. She began to work with the American Foundation for the Blind in 1924 and served as its chief fund-raiser until her death in 1968, at the age of 87.

1. **Recognizing Words in Context**

Find the word *pacifist* in the passage. One definition below is closest to the meaning of that word. One definition has the opposite or nearly the opposite meaning. The remaining definition has a completely different meaning. Label the definitions C for *closest*, O for *opposite or nearly opposite*, and D for *different*.

_____ a. patron

_____ b. warlike

_____ c. peace-loving

2. **Distinguishing Fact from Opinion**

Two of the statements below present *facts*, which can be proved. The other statement is an *opinion*, which expresses someone's thoughts or beliefs. Label the statements F for *fact* and O for *opinion*.

_____ a. Helen Keller did more for the American Foundation for the Blind than any other individual in history.

_____ b. Even though she was deaf, Helen Keller learned to speak.

_____ c. Helen Keller realized that many people had harder lives than she did.

3. Keeping Events in Order

Number the statements below 1, 2, and 3 to show the order in which the events took place.

_____ a. Keller attended Radcliffe College.

_____ b. Keller became a spokesperson for the American Foundation for the Blind.

_____ c. Keller joined the Socialist Party.

4. Making Correct Inferences

Two of the statements below are correct *inferences,* or reasonable guesses. They are based on information in the passage. The other statement is an incorrect, or faulty, inference. Label the statements C for *correct* inference and F for *faulty* inference.

_____ a. Keller's own blindness helped make her an effective spokesperson for the rights of the blind.

_____ b. Keller would have achieved even more in her life had she not been such an unruly child.

_____ c. The blind and others with disabilities are sometimes treated unfairly.

5. Understanding Main Ideas

One of the statements below expresses the main idea of the passage. One statement is too general, or too broad. The other explains only part of the passage; it is too narrow. Label the statements M for *main idea*, B for *too broad*, and N for *too narrow*.

_____ a. People with disabilities are capable of great achievements.

_____ b. Helen Keller spoke out for the rights of women, children, workers, and minorities.

_____ c. Helen Keller overcame significant disabilities to become a woman of remarkable achievements.

Correct Answers, Part A _____

Correct Answers, Part B _____

Total Correct Answers _____

The Russians and the Aleuts

In the late 1700s, Russian explorers became the first Europeans to land on the group of islands that extend in an east-west arc from the Alaskan Peninsula. Today, these islands are known as the Aleutians. The Native peoples that the Russians encountered are the Aleuts. The islands' environment was rich, yet often harsh, and centered around the sea. The lives of the people, who called themselves Unangan, were shaped and defined by their dependence on the seals, whales, and sea otters that abounded there. Ironically it was the Russians' shared interest in these sea mammals that destroyed the Unangan way of life.

At the time of the Russians' arrival, about 15 thousand Unangan made these islands their home. They lived in villages of various sizes. The larger villages were located close to salmon streams and were made up of large communal houses called *ulaxes*. Ulaxes, which were built partially underground, could be 200 feet long or longer. Unangan society was organized into social classes consisting of enslaved people, common folk, and nobility. Archaeological evidence suggests that this social structure had existed since about 1200.

The Unangan were skilled hunters of sea mammals. They harpooned their quarry from sturdy, flexible, kayak-like boats called *iqats*. An iqat had a frame made of shaped driftwood bound with sinew, bone, and baleen (whalebone). The frame was covered with sealskin and coated with watertight layers of seal oil. In search of their prey, hunters performed many elaborate rituals in preparation for each hunt.

Sea animals provided most of the products the Unangan needed to survive. Women sewed warm, waterproof garments of skin and seal gut. Seal meat was an important part of the Unangan's diet. They also gathered shellfish, sea grasses, and kelp, and they picked berries.

The Unangan's boat-handling and hunting skills left the Russians awestruck. Unable to master these skills themselves, the Russians forced Unangan hunters to hunt for them. When the Unangan resisted, the Russians, armed with rifles (which the Unangan lacked), killed these Native people. The Russians also kidnapped Unangan wives and children, returning them at the end of the hunting season—if at all. Unangan women and children became malnourished without the meat and skins they were used to. Within 50 years after the Russians' arrival, two-thirds or more of the Unangan population had died as a result of starvation, disease, and war.

Reading Time _____

Recalling Facts

1. The people of the Aleutian Islands called themselves
   - ❏ a. Ulaxes.
   - ❏ b. Aleuts.
   - ❏ c. Unangan.

2. The Unangan's boat, the iqat, was
   - ❏ a. large.
   - ❏ b. heavy.
   - ❏ c. flexible.

3. Unangan society was
   - ❏ a. egalitarian.
   - ❏ b. made up of hunting and gathering groups.
   - ❏ c. organized into classes of enslaved people, common people, and nobility.

4. Thousands of Unangan died in the decades after the Russians arrived as a result of
   - ❏ a. disease, war, and starvation.
   - ❏ b. hunting accidents, war, and disease.
   - ❏ c. the extinction of seals, disease, and starvation.

5. Archaeologists believe that the Unangan social structure in the 1700s dates back to about
   - ❏ a. the late 1600s.
   - ❏ b. 1200.
   - ❏ c. 15,000 B.C.

Understanding Ideas

6. The Unangan could not successfully resist the Russians mainly because
   - ❏ a. the Russians had better weapons.
   - ❏ b. they believed that the Russians were of the nobility.
   - ❏ c. they did not believe in violence.

7. One could conclude that
   - ❏ a. Europeans in the 1700s generally respected Native people's rights.
   - ❏ b. the skills that enabled the Unangan to survive in their environment led to their enslavement by the Russians.
   - ❏ c. the Unangan's overdependence on the sea meant that they were unequipped to fight effectively on land.

8. One can conclude that the author probably thinks the Russians' behavior toward the Unangan was
   - ❏ a. justified.
   - ❏ b. ruthless.
   - ❏ c. appropriate for that time.

9. The Unangan probably located some villages close to salmon streams because
   - ❏ a. salmon were a good source of food.
   - ❏ b. Unangan hunters used salmon as bait for catching seals.
   - ❏ c. the streams were the only source of drinking water.

10. The harshness of the Unangan's environment was probably a result of
    - ❏ a. lack of rainfall.
    - ❏ b. cold arctic conditions.
    - ❏ c. rough seas.

At first contact between the Russians and the Unangan, the Pribilof Islands were uninhabited. Located about two hundred miles north of the Aleutian chain, they were known only in legend as the breeding grounds of the fur seal. In 1786 the Russians found this valuable source of furs for the European market. They forcibly relocated Aleut hunters to the islands and put them to work killing seals.

The Aleuts began life on the Pribilofs as slave labor, but eventually, they gained the rights of Russian subjects. They were paid fair wages and were able to maintain their traditional culture and some self-rule. But in 1867, after the United States bought the Alaskan Territory, conditions worsened. The Aleuts lost their rights and became an exploited labor force. They harvested seals for meager wages, and the U.S. government took the profits from the sale of furs. This situation continued until the United States abandoned the trade in 1983. With this loss of their only source of income, the Aleuts suffered even worse poverty. They received $20 million from the U.S. government and used the money to develop new sources of livelihood. Today the Pribilof Aleuts have successful halibut- and crab-fishing industries. They have also begun programs to reacquaint their young people with traditional ways and encourage preservation of the environment.

1. **Recognizing Words in Context**

   Find the word *meager* in the passage. One definition below is closest to the meaning of that word. One definition has the opposite or nearly the opposite meaning. The remaining definition has a completely different meaning. Label the definitions C for *closest*, O for *opposite or nearly opposite*, and D for *different*.

   _____ a. untaxed

   _____ b. skimpy

   _____ c. generous

2. **Distinguishing Fact from Opinion**

   Two of the statements below present *facts*, which can be proved. The other statement is an *opinion*, which expresses someone's thoughts or beliefs. Label the statements F for *fact* and O for *opinion*.

   _____ a. The seal-fur trade on the Pribilofs was profitable for almost 200 years.

   _____ b. The U.S. government gave the Pribilof Aleuts only $20 million.

   _____ c. The original inhabitants of the Pribilofs were forced to work there.

3. Keeping Events in Order

Number the statements below 1, 2, and 3 to show the order in which the events took place.

_____ a. The Russians discovered the Pribilof Islands.

_____ b. The U.S. government pulled out of the seal-fur trade.

_____ c. The Pribilof Aleuts developed halibut- and crab-fishing industries.

4. Making Correct Inferences

Two of the statements below are correct *inferences,* or reasonable guesses. They are based on information in the passage. The other statement is an incorrect, or faulty, inference. Label the statements C for *correct* inference and F for *faulty* inference.

_____ a. The Pribilof Aleuts could have left the islands if they had wanted to.

_____ b. The Pribilof Aleuts value their traditional culture.

_____ c. The economy of the Pribilof Islands depends to a large extent on the natural environment.

5. Understanding Main Ideas

One of the statements below expresses the main idea of the passage. One statement is too general, or too broad. The other explains only part of the passage; it is too narrow. Label the statements M for *main idea*, B for *too broad,* and N for *too narrow*.

_____ a. The Pribilof Aleuts had problems after the United States pulled out of the seal-fur industry.

_____ b. Over the course of 200 years, the Pribilof Aleuts developed from an exploited people into the managers of a successful fishing industry.

_____ c. The Pribilof Aleut culture has adapted to many of the challenges presented to them in the last two centuries.

Correct Answers, Part A _____

Correct Answers, Part B _____

Total Correct Answers _____

Of all types of maps available, a globe can show distances, areas, directions, and shapes most closely to the way they actually exist on Earth's surface. However, for practical purposes, flat maps present obvious advantages over globes. They can be folded up and stored or carried around easily. Because they can be drawn to large scales, which would not be practical for globes, they can show small details.

Cartographers have developed various mathematical means, called projections, of translating images of Earth's curved surface into a flat form. Projections are calculated mathematically, but they work something like this: Imagine a light inside a globe projecting an image of Earth's surface onto a piece of paper wrapped around the globe. Depending on how this imaginary piece of paper touches or is wrapped around the globe, one of three basic types of map projections results. *Planar* projections are produced as though the imaginary piece of paper touches Earth at one point. (The *gnomonic* projection, believed to have been developed by the Greek mathematician Thales in the 500s B.C., is a planar projection.) *Conical* projections are produced as though the paper were formed into a cone and perched on the globe. *Cylindrical* map projections are drawn as if the paper were wrapped around the globe to form a cylinder.

Although flat maps are of much practical use, their usefulness comes at a price—distortion. In other words, a map can show true distances, true directions, true areas, or true shapes, but never all four. *Conformal* maps, for example, show true shapes, but sizes are distorted. *Equal-area projections* show the correct sizes of areas in relation to one another, but shapes are distorted. Distortions result from the shrinking, slicing, and stretching that must occur when a spherical Earth is shown on a flat surface. Map users choose the map projection that produces the least distortion in the feature that is most important for their specific purpose. Planar projections are useful for mapping polar areas. Because of its shape and size, the United States can be mapped with fair accuracy by using a conical projection. The *Robinson* projection falls into no single category of projections. It is, in effect, a compromise projection because it has some distortion in each major feature, but it gives a picture of Earth's land masses that is close to reality. This quality makes it a popular map for use in teaching geography.

Reading Time _____

Recalling Facts

1. The only type of map that can show distance, area, direction, and shape more-or-less accurately is a
   - ❏ a. globe.
   - ❏ b. conic projection.
   - ❏ c. Robinson world map.

2. A mathematical means of translating Earth's surface onto a flat map is called a
   - ❏ a. distortion.
   - ❏ b. conformal map.
   - ❏ c. projection.

3. Polar areas can be accurately mapped by using a
   - ❏ a. conical projection.
   - ❏ b. planar projection.
   - ❏ c. cylindrical projection.

4. The three basic types of map projections are the
   - ❏ a. planar, conical, and cylindrical.
   - ❏ b. conformal, equal-area, and conical.
   - ❏ c. Robinson, gnomonic, and planar.

5. Cartographers make flat maps by
   - ❏ a. wrapping paper around a globe and projecting the images onto it.
   - ❏ b. peeling images from a globe like an orange rind and then flattening them.
   - ❏ c. using mathematical formulas to translate Earth's curved surface onto a flat surface.

Understanding Ideas

6. The chief challenge of mapmaking is
   - ❏ a. eliminating distortion in polar regions.
   - ❏ b. translating the curved surface of Earth onto flat paper.
   - ❏ c. providing the small details that are needed by travelers.

7. A map that shows true directions
   - ❏ a. cannot be a cylindrical projection.
   - ❏ b. probably cannot also show true areas, distances, and shapes.
   - ❏ c. can only be a globe because it can show distances, areas, directions, and shapes most closely to the way they actually exist.

8. The type of map that is most accurate in showing the shapes and positions of continents is a
   - ❏ a. planar map.
   - ❏ b. gnomonic map.
   - ❏ c. Robinson projection map.

9. One can conclude that
   - ❏ a. if globes could be made to a large-enough scale, they would be more useful than maps.
   - ❏ b. maps that show a large portion of Earth's surface have more distortion than maps showing small areas.
   - ❏ c. the most useful and practical maps are very difficult to acquire.

10. From the passage, one can conclude that making projection maps
    - ❏ a. is no longer relevant.
    - ❏ b. has been done since ancient times.
    - ❏ c. is futile because no map has ever been completely accurate.

In the late 1400s, increasingly fast, sturdy ships made long-distance voyages possible for European seafarers. The maps available at that time, however, were inadequate for plotting courses over long distances. Maps were drawn as if places were connected by curved lines. This was done to replicate the way places are situated on Earth's surface. As a result, sailors had to calculate courses by using curved lines. Sailors who plotted a straight-line course toward their destination would end up somewhere else because of distortion. This situation can be compared to what happens when an arrow is aimed at a target far away. The archer cannot aim directly at the target because gravity causes the arrow's path to curve downward. The archer must aim above the target in order to hit it. The greater the distance, the greater the distortion.

Flemish cartographer Gerardus Mercator solved this problem in 1569. He devised a cylindrical map in which the curvature of directional lines is mathematically eliminated. There is no distortion of direction on a Mercator map. A straight line drawn anywhere on the map shows true direction. Using this map, sailors could calculate their courses across the ocean in straight lines instead of curves. Even though distance and area is distorted near the polar regions, these distortions were not important to sailors using the map.

1. **Recognizing Words in Context**

Find the word *replicate* in the passage. One definition below is closest to the meaning of that word. One definition has the opposite or nearly the opposite meaning. The remaining definition has a completely different meaning. Label the definitions C for *closest*, O for *opposite or nearly opposite*, and D for *different*.

_____ a. distort

_____ b. argue

_____ c. copy

2. **Distinguishing Fact from Opinion**

Two of the statements below present *facts*, which can be proved. The other statement is an *opinion*, which expresses someone's thoughts or beliefs. Label the statements F for *fact* and O for *opinion*.

_____ a. Mercator's map projection helped sailors to plot accurate courses at sea.

_____ b. Older maps worked well for relatively short voyages but not for long ones.

_____ c. Sailors would have stopped making long-distance trips without Mercator's map.

3. Keeping Events in Order

Number the statements below 1, 2, and 3 to show the order in which the events took place.

_____ a. Mercator developed his new map projection.

_____ b. Ships suitable for longer ocean voyages were developed.

_____ c. European sailors could plot their courses by drawing straight lines on maps.

4. Making Correct Inferences

Two of the statements below are correct *inferences,* or reasonable guesses. They are based on information in the passage. The other statement is an incorrect, or faulty, inference. Label the statements C for *correct* inference and F for *faulty* inference.

_____ a. To sailors navigating at sea, accurate information on direction is usually more important than accurate information on distance.

_____ b. Sailors were able to make long-distance voyages for many years without the aid of Mercator's map.

_____ c. Mercator maps were useful in the 1500s because sailors at that time never traveled to polar regions.

5. Understanding Main Ideas

One of the statements below expresses the main idea of the passage. One statement is too general, or too broad. The other explains only part of the passage; it is too narrow. Label the statements M for *main idea,* B for *too broad,* and N for *too narrow.*

_____ a. The Mercator map projection solved a navigation problem that arose when longer sea voyages became possible.

_____ b. Sailors use maps and charts as aids to navigation.

_____ c. Gerardus Mercator invented the Mercator map projection in 1569.

Correct Answers, Part A _____

Correct Answers, Part B _____

Total Correct Answers _____

The Electoral College

In the United States, most leaders are chosen by direct votes during political elections. In a direct vote, people cast ballots for the candidates of their choice. The winners are those who receive the most votes. The president, however is not elected by a direct vote of the people. The winner is decided through a majority vote in the Electoral College.

The Electoral College system was created by the U.S. Constitution. In this system, voters cast ballots for both electors and a presidential candidate. Then the electors choose the president. In 48 of the 50 states, the electors have to vote for the candidate who receives the most votes in that state. Except in Maine and Nebraska, it is largely a "winner takes all" system. Many have argued, in fact, that this process ignores the ballots cast by many voters.

The number of electors in each state equals the number of that state's members of Congress. No state has fewer than three electors, because each state has at least two senators and one representative. States with larger populations have more electors than those with fewer residents. In the year 2000, California, as the most populous state, had the most electors: 54. Seven states and the District of Columbia had just three electors. The system was designed to boost the voting power of smaller states. In 2000, for instance, there were about two and a half million eligible voters in five of the smallest states and the District of Columbia. Together they controlled 18 electoral votes. Michigan, by contrast, has more than seven million voting-age residents. It, too, controlled 18 electoral votes.

The Electoral College has one curious feature. It is possible for the candidate who wins the majority of the popular vote to lose the race in the Electoral College. How can this be? It is a matter of math and the "winner takes all" rule—especially important in a year when three or more candidates are running for president. The successful candidate in a state with less than half the popular vote can still control all of its electoral votes. The losing candidate can win most of the popular vote nationwide but lose in enough big states to lose the electoral vote.

Such was the case, for instance, in 1888 when Grover Cleveland lost to Benjamin Harrison and in 2000 when George W. Bush defeated Al Gore.

Reading Time _____

Recalling Facts

1. The president of the United States is elected by
   - ❏ a. the members of Congress.
   - ❏ b. a majority vote in the Electoral College.
   - ❏ c. a majority of voters who cast ballots.

2. The number of electors in each state
   - ❏ a. is the same throughout the country.
   - ❏ b. depends on the number of people registered to vote.
   - ❏ c. equals the number of that state's members of Congress.

3. In most states, the candidate with the majority of votes gets
   - ❏ a. three electoral votes.
   - ❏ b. all of the state's electoral votes.
   - ❏ c. the majority of the state's electoral votes.

4. The Electoral College system was designed to
   - ❏ a. boost the voting power of smaller states.
   - ❏ b. keep control of the elections out of the hands of the voters.
   - ❏ c. ensure that the most populous states would have the most influence.

5. In the presidential elections of 1888 and 2000, the candidate who won the
   - ❏ a. election won less than half the electoral vote.
   - ❏ b. popular vote lost the race in the Electoral College.
   - ❏ c. popular vote also won the vote in the Electoral College.

Understanding Ideas

6. One can conclude that each state
   - ❏ a. gives all of its electoral votes to the winning candidate.
   - ❏ b. gives a percentage of its electoral vote to each candidate.
   - ❏ c. decides how to use its electoral votes in a presidential election.

7. Those who designed the Electoral College probably believed that the
   - ❏ a. voters were not intelligent enough to elect a president.
   - ❏ b. the outcome of a presidential election needed to be a surprise.
   - ❏ c. interests of smaller states needed to be protected.

8. A "winner takes all" system could be said to ignore many of a state's voters, because it
   - ❏ a. favors weaker candidates.
   - ❏ b. favors third-party candidates.
   - ❏ c. does not reflect the true percentage of votes cast for the winning candidate.

9. On can infer from this passage that the number of representatives assigned to each state
   - ❏ a. depends on the state's wealth.
   - ❏ b. depends on the state's population.
   - ❏ c. is decided by the size of the state in square miles.

10. The Electoral College system is more likely to reflect the will of the people who vote when
    - ❏ a. there are only two candidates.
    - ❏ b. the president is the candidate running for reelection.
    - ❏ c. there are three or more presidential candidates.

The quirks of the Electoral College system have sometimes cast a cloud over election results. In 1824, for instance, four men vied for the office of president. Andrew Jackson won the largest share of both the popular and electoral votes. He did not, however, get a majority of either. Election rules required a decision from the House of Representatives. After deals were struck, John Quincy Adams was the choice for president in 13 out of the 24 states.

Many people were outraged. Jackson spent the next four years on the campaign trail. After four years, changes in many state laws worked to his benefit. More people had become eligible to vote. The choice of electors was taken away from most state legislatures and given to the voters. A number of local offices were changed from appointed ones to elected ones. A surge in voter fervor greatly increased turnout.

Jackson beat Adams in the 1828 election. He took 56 percent of the popular vote and two-thirds of the votes in the Electoral College. In 1832 Jackson was reelected by an even larger electoral margin.

Success in the Electoral College did not make Jackson like the system. As president he tried without success to eliminate the Electoral College system and change the way the president is chosen.

1. **Recognizing Words in Context**

   Find the word *fervor* in the passage. One definition below is closest to the meaning of that word. One definition has the opposite or nearly the opposite meaning. The remaining definition has a completely different meaning. Label the definitions C for *closest*, O for *opposite or nearly opposite*, and D for *different*.

   _____ a. peculiarity

   _____ b. enthusiasm

   _____ c. lack of interest

2. **Distinguishing Fact from Opinion**

   Two of the statements below present *facts*, which can be proved. The other statement is an *opinion*, which expresses someone's thoughts or beliefs. Label the statements F for *fact* and O for *opinion*.

   _____ a. John Quincy Adams's election in 1824 was unfair.

   _____ b. Members of the House of Representatives chose the president in 1824.

   _____ c. Andrew Jackson was unsuccessful in changing the way the president is chosen.

3. Keeping Events in Order

Number the statements below 1, 2, and 3 to show the order in which the events took place.

_____ a. No candidate wins a clear majority of votes in the Electoral College.

_____ b. Jackson serves two terms as president.

_____ c. Adams is named president by the House of Representatives.

4. Making Correct Inferences

Two of the statements below are correct *inferences*, or reasonable guesses. They are based on information in the passage. The other statement is an incorrect, or faulty, inference. Label the statements C for *correct* inference and F for *faulty* inference.

_____ a. If winning did not require a majority of electoral votes, Jackson would have won the presidency in 1824.

_____ b. Jackson was unfairly denied the presidency in 1824.

_____ c. When choosing a president is assigned to the House of Representatives, each state gets one vote.

5. Understanding Main Ideas

One of the statements below expresses the main idea of the passage. One statement is too general, or too broad. The other explains only part of the passage; it is too narrow. Label the statements M for *main idea*, B for *too broad*, and N for *too narrow*.

_____ a. The Electoral College system does not always ensure a clear winner in a presidential race.

_____ b. Andrew Jackson won the presidency in 1828 with two-thirds of the electoral votes.

_____ c. Andrew Jackson's dislike of the Electoral College system was intensified by his loss in the 1824 election.

Correct Answers, Part A _____

Correct Answers, Part B _____

Total Correct Answers _____

The sweet, juicy orange has come a long way from its original birthplace. The ancient orange was a bitter fruit. It probably became established in Southeast Asia about 20 million years ago. People began to develop the modern, or sweet, orange in Asia 5,000 to 6,000 years ago. Through the ages, careful tending changed this wild form into the tasty treat enjoyed today. Scholars are unsure where people first grew oranges for eating. However, China, India, Bhutan, Malaysia, and Burma are strong possibilities.

From Asia sweet oranges spread to North Africa and then to Spain and Portugal. European explorers planted orange trees in warm, humid parts of North and South America about 1500. Growers began raising oranges in Brazil about 1530. After many years, a sweet, thick-skinned, seedless orange grew naturally. What set this orange apart was a small lesser fruit, or navel, rooted in the top. This orange variety, called the Bahia orange, was discovered about 1800.

About 1870, a missionary in Brazil, impressed with the Bahia orange, sent some trees to the U.S. Department of Agriculture (USDA) in Washington, D.C. A couple named Eliza and Luther Tibbets, who had just moved to Riverside, California, wrote to the USDA for information on the kind of trees they should plant at their new home. The USDA was eager to learn whether the Bahia oranges were suited to California's climate, so it sent the Tibbetses three trees in 1873. People began to talk about the Tibbetses' delicious fruit, which became known as the Washington navel. The Tibbetses' oranges won awards for their outstanding flavor. Soon the Tibbetses were selling starter buds from their trees for five dollars each.

The navels thrived in the semidesert climate of Riverside. However, the amount of rain that fell was often short of the trees' needs. In 1885 Matthew Gage gave the region's orange crops a big boost when he completed a 12-mile-long irrigation canal. The canal diverted water from the Santa Ana River to the groves of Riverside.

About the turn of the century, word that fortunes could be made by growing and selling oranges began to spread. By 1910 California boasted about one hundred thousand acres of groves propagated from the Tibbetses' trees, which still stand in what is now downtown Riverside. Protected by wrought iron fences and named a California state historical landmark, they are a permanent tribute to the importance of the orange in California.

Reading Time _____

Recalling Facts

1. Ancient ancestors of today's oranges were
   - ❏ a. sour.
   - ❏ b. sweet.
   - ❏ c. bitter.

2. The first eating oranges were developed beginning about
   - ❏ a. five to six thousand years ago.
   - ❏ b. twenty million years ago.
   - ❏ c. the nineteenth century, at the Tibbetses' farm.

3. The Bahia orange first appeared in
   - ❏ a. China.
   - ❏ b. Brazil.
   - ❏ c. California.

4. Another name for the Bahia orange is the
   - ❏ a. Luther orange.
   - ❏ b. Washington navel orange.
   - ❏ c. California flavorful orange.

5. The U.S. Department of Agriculture wanted to know whether
   - ❏ a. Washington navel oranges would sell.
   - ❏ b. the Tibbetses could manage a farm.
   - ❏ c. the Bahia orange would grow in California.

Understanding Ideas

6. The navel orange got its name from
   - ❏ a. sailors who brought it back from their journeys.
   - ❏ b. people who could not pronounce the name *Bahia*.
   - ❏ c. the small secondary fruit embedded in the main fruit.

7. One can conclude that the start of the orange industry in California
   - ❏ a. was an accident.
   - ❏ b. was the result of a process of orange cultivation carried on for centuries throughout the world.
   - ❏ c. took a long time because people did not like eating oranges.

8. The information in the passage suggests that it is unlikely that oranges could survive in
   - ❏ a. coastal areas.
   - ❏ b. cold climates.
   - ❏ c. dry and hot regions.

9. One of the reasons the Tibbetses could sell their starter buds for such a high price may have been that
   - ❏ a. no seeds were available.
   - ❏ b. the USDA would make the trees available only to the Tibbetses.
   - ❏ c. no more trees could be imported from Brazil.

10. The trait that most suited the Washington navel to dry conditions was probably its
    - ❏ a. color.
    - ❏ b. sweetness.
    - ❏ c. thick skin.

Hazardous Harvests

California produces about four-fifths of the United States' table oranges, or oranges meant for eating. Most jobs related to the industry are done by Hispanic farm workers. They prune trees, apply pesticides and fertilizers, and pick the oranges by hand. In the fields, the workers pack the fruit in 50-pound boxes. At the packinghouses, other workers inspect, sort, and pack the oranges in shipping cartons.

The jobs provide scant income, little security, and major risks. The workers earn about six to eight dollars an hour, and few receive medical coverage. They sometimes climb ladders 18 to 20 feet high to reach the tops of trees. Falls are not uncommon. Because oranges are vulnerable to pests such as insects and worms, pesticides are applied. Orange production is second only to grape production in the rate of pesticide poisonings of workers. Although there are mandates in California to protect workers, laborers may be affected while applying the pesticides and while harvesting and packing the fruit.

Between 13,000 and 15,000 workers depend on the winter citrus harvest in the San Joaquin Valley. Some entire communities in the Central Valley also depend on the orange crop for their livelihood. In 1990 and 1998, freezes destroyed much of the citrus crop. Pickers and packinghouse workers had no work, and many families suffered great hardship.

1. Recognizing Words in Context

Find the word *vulnerable* in the passage. One definition below is closest to the meaning of that word. One definition has the opposite or nearly the opposite meaning. The remaining definition has a completely different meaning. Label the definitions C for *closest,* O for *opposite or nearly opposite,* and D for *different.*

_____ a. safe

_____ b. expensive

_____ c. exposed

2. Distinguishing Fact from Opinion

Two of the statements below present *facts,* which can be proved. The other statement is an *opinion,* which expresses someone's thoughts or beliefs. Label the statements F for *fact* and O for *opinion.*

_____ a. Orange workers risk poisoning by pesticides.

_____ b. Entire communities in the Central Valley depend on the orange industry for their livelihood.

_____ c. Pesticides should never be applied to the foods that people eat.

3. Keeping Events in Order

Number the statements below 1, 2, and 3 to show the order in which the events took place.

_____ a. Workers inspect oranges at the packinghouse.

_____ b. Workers harvest oranges by hand.

_____ c. Workers pack oranges in 50-pound boxes in the fields.

4. Making Correct Inferences

Two of the statements below are correct *inferences,* or reasonable guesses. They are based on information in the passage. The other statement is an incorrect, or faulty, inference. Label the statements C for *correct* inference and F for *faulty* inference.

_____ a. High health risks drive most farm laborers away from the orange industry.

_____ b. Oranges are vulnerable to damage by pests.

_____ c. A good orange crop means work not only for harvesters but for packing-house employees as well.

5. Understanding Main Ideas

One of the statements below expresses the main idea of the passage. One statement is too general, or too broad. The other explains only part of the passage; it is too narrow. Label the statements M for *main idea,* B for *too broad,* and N for *too narrow.*

_____ a. Oranges are vulnerable to pests, such as insects and worms, and to cold weather, such as the freeze in 1998 that destroyed much of central California's citrus crop.

_____ b. Many laborers depend on the orange industry, even though the pay is low and the work can be dangerous.

_____ c. Produce industries in California provide many jobs.

Correct Answers, Part A _____

Correct Answers, Part B _____

Total Correct Answers _____

The Birth of Credit and Debt

For as long as people have desired goods that they could not afford, there has been credit and debt. Records date back to the ancient city-states of Mesopotamia, in what is now Iraq. In the 3000s B.C., the practice of lending and borrowing worked much as it does today.

The discovery that money grows in value over time marked the beginning of modern credit-and-debt arrangements. Historians believe that ancient Mesopotamian herders first made this connection. They observed that when one livestock owner lent a herd to another, at least some of the animals would give birth during the time of the loan. To make up for that natural growth, the borrower would have to return more livestock than were originally lent. Sometime in the 2000s B.C., people learned to apply the same principle to other goods and to money. The concept of interest was born. When one person lent another person silver, for example, the lender would charge a certain percentage of the amount in interest over time. The interest rate was based in part on how much that silver would have increased in value had the lender used it to carry on business or make investments.

In the 1920s, the ruins of a financial district were found in the Mesopotamian city of Ur. Stone tablets show that lively lending and borrowing took place there in the 1800s and 1700s B.C. Merchants borrowed silver from one another to fund new businesses. Some individuals acted as banks. They paid depositors a small amount of interest. Then they used the money for their own ventures. They used it to set up a new business, to invest in the businesses of others, or to make loans at higher interest rates.

Such shifting of funds kept money flowing into new businesses and added to the country's wealth and productivity, but it put great pressure on poor people who had to borrow money for emergency purposes. Lenders charged high interest rates for these short-term loans. Those who could not pay back their debts often had to sell themselves or family members into slavery. Sometimes, however, the tables would be turned on the lenders. Rulers occasionally announced kingdomwide forgiveness of debt. Such announcements were a blessing for debtors, but they spelled financial ruin for lenders. Scholars believe that such a declaration, issued by King Rim-Sin in 1788 B.C., brought about a financial crash from which the city of Ur never recovered.

Reading Time _____

Recalling Facts

1. The earliest records of credit and debt date back to the
   - ❏ a. 1800s B.C.
   - ❏ b. 2000s B.C.
   - ❏ c. 3000s B.C.

2. The percentage of a loan amount that is charged to an account for the growth of the money over time is called
   - ❏ a. debt.
   - ❏ b. interest.
   - ❏ c. investment.

3. Remains of a financial district were found in the ruins of the ancient city of
   - ❏ a. Ur.
   - ❏ b. Rim-Sin.
   - ❏ c. Mesopotamia.

4. Historians think that ancient Mesopotamians discovered the relationship of time and money by observing how
   - ❏ a. livestock multiplied.
   - ❏ b. loans were provided.
   - ❏ c. interest added up over time.

5. Poor people often had to sell themselves into slavery because
   - ❏ a. their businesses failed.
   - ❏ b. the king forgave the lenders.
   - ❏ c. they could not repay their debts.

Understanding Ideas

6. A drawback of widespread credit and debt was that it
   - ❏ a. made money unavailable.
   - ❏ b. led to higher interest rates.
   - ❏ c. created hardship for poor people.

7. One conclusion that can be drawn from this passage is that
   - ❏ a. money automatically grows in value over time.
   - ❏ b. debt causes hardship for some people and creates opportunities for others.
   - ❏ c. interest rates that lenders charge are always fair.

8. An individual acts as a bank when he or she
   - ❏ a. starts a business.
   - ❏ b. forgives another person's debt.
   - ❏ c. borrows money and then lends it to someone else.

9. Debt forgiveness spelled financial ruin for lenders because
   - ❏ a. it meant that they would never be paid back the money they were owed.
   - ❏ b. people would no longer invest in lenders' businesses or any other businesses they started.
   - ❏ c. lenders often needed to sell themselves and their families into slavery in order to survive.

10. A benefit of borrowing and lending in ancient Mesopotamia was that it
    - ❏ a. kept money flowing into new businesses.
    - ❏ b. led to kingdomwide debt forgiveness in 1788 B.C.
    - ❏ c. made money available at extremely high interest rates.

Credit cards can make life easier or cause harm. It all depends on how they are used.

Because the terms of credit cards vary greatly, smart users know how they plan to use a card before they apply for one. A person who plans to use a credit card to finance purchases generally chooses a card with a low interest rate. Another may use a card to avoid carrying cash. He or she usually pays off the balance every month. In this case, a card with no annual fee and a grace period is best. The grace period is a period of days or weeks between the time of purchase and the time the payment is due, during which no interest is charged.

A shrewd user examines statements carefully, compares the balance to funds available, and pays off as much of the balance as possible. Many people get into financial trouble with credit cards because they do not realize how quickly finance charges can add up. If they pay only the minimum amount each month and continue to add to the debt, they can find themselves in serious financial difficulty. They can recover from the problem by not using their cards until they can pay off most or all of every balance.

1. **Recognizing Words in Context**

   Find the word *shrewd* in the passage. One definition below is closest to the meaning of that word. One definition has the opposite or nearly the opposite meaning. The remaining definition has a completely different meaning. Label the definitions C for *closest,* O for *opposite or nearly opposite,* and D for *different.*

   _____ a. unwise

   _____ b. resourceful

   _____ c. wealthy

2. **Distinguishing Fact from Opinion**

   Two of the statements below present *facts,* which can be proved. The other statement is an *opinion,* which expresses someone's thoughts or beliefs. Label the statements F for *fact* and O for *opinion.*

   _____ a. The terms of credit cards vary greatly.

   _____ b. Paying off the balance in full every month is the only sensible way to use a credit card.

   _____ c. Not paying attention to finance charges is one way people get into financial trouble with credit cards.

3. Keeping Events in Order

Number the statements below 1, 2, and 3 to show the order in which the events took place.

_____ a. The credit-card user examines the bill as soon as it arrives.

_____ b. The credit-card user pays off as much of the balance as possible.

_____ c. The credit-card user decides how he or she will use the credit card.

4. Making Correct Inferences

Two of the statements below are correct *inferences,* or reasonable guesses. They are based on information in the passage. The other statement is an incorrect, or faulty, inference. Label the statements C for *correct* inference and F for *faulty* inference.

_____ a. The higher the interest rate charged, the faster the debt can pile up.

_____ b. People have many choices in both the type of credit cards they choose and in how they use them.

_____ c. There is a perfect credit card for every user.

5. Understanding Main Ideas

One of the statements below expresses the main idea of the passage. One statement is too general, or too broad. The other explains only part of the passage; it is too narrow. Label the statements M for *main idea,* B for *too broad,* and N for *too narrow.*

_____ a. Credit cards can be helpful or damaging depending upon how they are used.

_____ b. A credit card is one of many useful tools.

_____ c. A card with a grace period charges no interest between the time of purchase and the time the payment is due.

Correct Answers, Part A _____

Correct Answers, Part B _____

Total Correct Answers _____

Gandhi and Nehru: Shared Goals, Opposing Values

The two chief figures in India's struggle for independence from British rule, Mohandas K. Gandhi and Jawaharlal Nehru, liked and respected each other. Despite their shared goals, however, their visions of an independent India differed in several ways. In the end, neither man's hope for his country was fully realized.

Gandhi gained leadership of the Quit-India movement with his method of social change called *satyagraha,* or "truth force." Nonviolent resistance to British rule, said Gandhi, was the right way to gain independence. Acts of violence would only be met with greater violence. Peaceful refusal to submit to injustice, on the other hand, would show the British that the Indians' cause was just. The power of nonviolence would lead the British to leave the country willingly.

Gandhi wanted India to become a nation in which spirituality was the highest good. Indian life would be focused on small villages. There, simple means of livelihood, such as farming and the spinning of cloth, would be prevalent. People would take care of their own and treat one another fairly. Without pressure to create wealth, they would be free to grow spiritually. To Gandhi it was vital that India avoid the ways of Western industrial society, which he believed were based on greed and robbed people of their dignity.

Inspired by Gandhi's leadership, Nehru quickly became one of his most loyal followers. Their partnership grew despite the fact that Nehru called Gandhi's vision for India "completely unreal." Nehru valued technology and wanted India to become a modern world power. He shared Gandhi's hatred of social injustice. However, his solution was not to reject the production of wealth but to ensure that the wealth was shared fairly among the entire population.

India achieved independence in 1947. Nehru became the country's first prime minister. Less than a year later, Gandhi was dead, killed by an assassin. His legacy of nonviolent resistance to social injustice would inspire future leaders such as Martin Luther King Jr., in the United States. During his almost 20 years in office, Nehru was able to guide India to a powerful position on the world stage under a democratic, parliamentary system of government. However, Nehru met with many social and political obstacles to his economic programs. As a result, many of the problems that both he and Gandhi had believed could be solved by independence—poverty, hunger, and disease—remained.

Reading Time _____

Recalling Facts

1. Gandhi's method of protest against British rule was based on
   - ❏ a. nonviolence.
   - ❏ b. modernization.
   - ❏ c. transferring power to the village level.

2. Nehru thought that wealth
   - ❏ a. led to greed.
   - ❏ b. was a necessary evil.
   - ❏ c. should be distributed equally among all Indian people.

3. Nehru became India's first
   - ❏ a. president.
   - ❏ b. prime minister.
   - ❏ c. independence leader.

4. India achieved independence in
   - ❏ a. 1927.
   - ❏ b. 1937.
   - ❏ c. 1947.

5. *Satyagraha* means
   - ❏ a. hope.
   - ❏ b. truth force.
   - ❏ c. social change.

Understanding Ideas

6. From the passage one can conclude that the struggle for Indian independence
   - ❏ a. was easily won.
   - ❏ b. required discipline and sacrifice.
   - ❏ c. called for military superiority.

7. The main difference between Nehru's and Gandhi's beliefs involved each man's ideas about
   - ❏ a. why British rule was unjust.
   - ❏ b. how liberation from the British should be accomplished.
   - ❏ c. what the roles of technology and modernization should be after achieving independence.

8. In comparing Gandhi's and Nehru's visions for India, one might say that
   - ❏ a. Gandhi wanted peace, and Nehru saw war as the answer.
   - ❏ b. Gandhi primarily sought spiritual development, and Nehru primarily sought material development.
   - ❏ c. Gandhi resisted imperial rule, and Nehru fought for personal power.

9. It is likely that Nehru would have compared Gandhi's vision of life in India after independence to
   - ❏ a. wishful thinking.
   - ❏ b. Western society.
   - ❏ c. a spinning wheel.

10. Gandhi's belief that his concept of *satyagraha* would be successful suggests that he saw the British as
    - ❏ a. cruel monsters.
    - ❏ b. greedy and selfish.
    - ❏ c. basically sensible.

Celebrating Independence

Throughout history, many countries gained their freedom only after long, hard, and often bloody struggles against a foreign power. For this reason, nations around the world often mark the anniversary of their independence with rousing celebrations that may include parades, fireworks displays, flag flying, and official holidays.

Countries often add to their celebrations elements that have special meaning. Mexico celebrates its independence day, September 16, with the battle cry *"Mexicanos, viva México!"* and the ringing of church bells. On this day in 1810, the Roman Catholic priest Miguel Hidalgo y Costillo rang his parish bell to call the people to Mass. Then, crying these words, he urged them to fight for their freedom from Spain. Mexicans did not win their freedom until 1821, but they still mark this day as the beginning of the end for Spanish rule.

In India many people celebrate their independence day by flying kites. The soaring kites represent the freedom that they won when, on August 15, 1947, the British gave up rule of India. Finland, in contrast, remembers its struggle for freedom with a more solemn rite. Each December 6, the day in 1917 on which Finland declared its independence from Russia, Finlanders attend formal dances, and many display two candles in their windows to pay tribute to those who fought during World War II.

1. **Recognizing Words in Context**

Find the word *rousing* in the passage. One definition below is closest to the meaning of that word. One definition has the opposite or nearly the opposite meaning. The remaining definition has a completely different meaning. Label the definitions C for *closest*, O for *opposite or nearly opposite*, and D for *different*.

_____ a. patriotic

_____ b. calm

_____ c. exciting

2. **Distinguishing Fact from Opinion**

Two of the statements below present *facts*, which can be proved. The other statement is an *opinion*, which expresses someone's thoughts or beliefs. Label the statements F for *fact* and O for *opinion*.

_____ a. Soaring kites are an inspiring symbol of freedom.

_____ b. The Mexicans fought 11 years for their independence.

_____ c. Parades and fireworks are typical of many countries' independence day celebrations.

3. Keeping Events in Order

Number the statements below 1, 2, and 3 to show the order in which the events took place.

_____ a. Father Hidalgo rang the church bells.

_____ b. The Indians heard the battle cry *"Mexicanos, viva México!"*

_____ c. Mexico won independence from Spain.

4. Making Correct Inferences

Two of the statements below are correct *inferences,* or reasonable guesses. They are based on information in the passage. The other statement is an incorrect, or faulty, inference. Label the statements C for *correct* inference and F for *faulty* inference.

_____ a. People generally value their country's independence and freedom.

_____ b. If the citizens of a country do not celebrate their independence, they will forget their history.

_____ c. The date of celebration of independence usually commemorates a specific historical event.

5. Understanding Main Ideas

One of the statements below expresses the main idea of the passage. One statement is too general, or too broad. The other explains only part of the passage; it is too narrow. Label the statements M for *main idea,* B for *too broad,* and N for *too narrow.*

_____ a. Mexico celebrates its independence day holiday, September 16, with the battle cry *"Mexicanos, viva México!"* and the ringing of church bells.

_____ b. Most countries of the world hold celebrations in remembrance of important events in their history.

_____ c. Independence celebrations often combine some common elements with others that are unique to a country's history.

Correct Answers, Part A _____

Correct Answers, Part B _____

Total Correct Answers _____

Sputnik Sparks the Space Race

In 1957 the Soviet Union launched the first artificial satellite into space. Its name was *Sputnik 1,* from the Russian word for *satellite.* Not much bigger than a basketball, *Sputnik* weighed less than 200 pounds. As it orbited Earth, it sent back radio signals that sounded like a cricket's chirps.

At the time of *Sputnik's* launch, the United States and Soviet Union were engaged in the Cold War, which began after World War II ended. The Soviet Union had taken control of much of Eastern Europe. It became a superpower that competed with the United States. Each nation built up a supply of arms to defend itself from the other. The two nations also competed in space. The Cold War ended when the Charter of Paris for a New Europe was signed in 1990.

Both the United States and the Soviet Union had said that they planned to put a satellite into orbit in 1957. The Soviet Union did it first, giving it an early lead in the space race. It claimed that *Sputnik's* launch proved the superiority of communism over capitalism.

The name of *Sputnik's* builder was kept a secret until after his death in 1966. He was known only as its "chief designer." Sergei Pavlovich Korolev was one of many aerospace engineers imprisoned from 1937 to 1938 by Soviet premier Josef Stalin. He was released in 1938 to help develop weapons.

Korolev's dream was to build a rocket that could put a person on the moon; but the Soviet government had little interest in space exploration. Therefore, Korolev proposed that they launch a satellite to test the working of instruments in space. He pointed out that the satellite could also be used to collect military information about the United States.

Korolev's team began working on a satellite called *Object D.* They planned to fill it with equipment to study the atmosphere, Earth's magnetic fields, and the Sun. Then Korolev learned that the United States was testing a three-stage missile. His team decided to build a smaller, simpler satellite. Ten months later, they sent *Sputnik* into orbit.

The United States won the race to land a person on the moon, but *Sputnik's* legacy endures. Its technology is now shared by the United States and Russia, partners in building the International Space Station. Other advances inspired by *Sputnik* include heart monitors, microelectronics used in computers, and the computer network that has become the Internet.

Reading Time _____

Recalling Facts

1. *Sputnik 1* was launched during
   - ❏ a. World War II.
   - ❏ b. the Cold War.
   - ❏ c. the Vietnam War.

2. *Sputnik 1* was the first
   - ❏ a. spy plane.
   - ❏ b. three-stage rocket.
   - ❏ c. constructed satellite.

3. *Sputnik 1* proved that
   - ❏ a. radio signals could be sent from space.
   - ❏ b. dogs could survive in space capsules.
   - ❏ c. human beings could survive reentry into Earth's atmosphere.

4. *Sputnik's* chief designer was
   - ❏ a. Werner von Braun.
   - ❏ b. Sergei Pavlovich Korolev.
   - ❏ c. Josef Stalin.

5. In the space race, *Sputnik* gave the Soviet Union
   - ❏ a. an early lead.
   - ❏ b. an embarrassing loss.
   - ❏ c. final victory.

Understanding Ideas

6. One can conclude that the Soviets
   - ❏ a. did not regard the United States as a serious rival in space.
   - ❏ b. were determined to reach Jupiter before the United States did.
   - ❏ c. considered *Sputnik* an important propaganda victory.

7. The Soviet government probably funded *Sputnik* because it wanted to
   - ❏ a. gain a military advantage.
   - ❏ b. repay Korolev for his unjust imprisonment.
   - ❏ c. explore the solar system.

8. One effect of the end of the Cold War is that the United States
   - ❏ a. claimed victory in the space race.
   - ❏ b. could spend more money on space exploration.
   - ❏ c. began working with the Soviet Union to explore space.

9. One can conclude that Korolev built a small satellite because he
   - ❏ a. wanted to be the first to send a satellite into orbit.
   - ❏ b. did not have enough money to build a big one.
   - ❏ c. knew that his rocket could launch only small objects.

10. The passage suggests that the technology developed for *Sputnik*
    - ❏ a. is less important than many historians believe.
    - ❏ b. is humankind's most significant achievement in space.
    - ❏ c. inspired different applications and the development of related technologies.

The launch of *Sputnik* in 1957 changed the way Americans learn science. Up to that time, the United States had been thought to have the best technology in the world. However, *Sputnik* showed that the Soviet Union was winning the space race. The satellite's orbit around the world also spread fears. People were worried that the Soviets could direct atomic bombs from space.

The United States quickly formed the National Aeronautics and Space Administration (NASA). However, more scientists and engineers were needed to win the space race. Science education was now paramount in the nation's defense.

The National Defense Education Act, passed in 1958, funded loans for students who were training for careers in science. High school students were required to take more science classes. The courses became more challenging. Even grade school students studied more math and science. Outdated textbooks were replaced with new books that covered more current theories.

Reformers also made changes in the way science was taught. Teachers began to stress principles instead of isolated facts. Hands-on activities gave students a chance to think like scientists. The new focus on "hard" science, however, meant that students spent less time exploring ways that science affects people's lives and their beliefs about scientific facts.

1. **Recognizing Words in Context**

   Find the word *paramount* in the passage. One definition below is closest to the meaning of that word. One definition has the opposite or nearly the opposite meaning. The remaining definition has a completely different meaning. Label the definitions C for *closest*, O for *opposite or nearly opposite,* and D for *different*.

   _____ a. uppermost

   _____ b. impersonal

   _____ c. insignificant

2. **Distinguishing Fact from Opinion**

   Two of the statements below present *facts*, which can be proved. The other statement is an *opinion*, which expresses someone's thoughts or beliefs. Label the statements F for *fact* and O for *opinion*.

   _____ a. *Sputnik* was launched in 1957.

   _____ b. Raising the science and math standards was an unfair decision.

   _____ c. American science books were updated after *Sputnik's* launch.

3. **Keeping Events in Order**

Number the statements below 1, 2, and 3 to show the order in which the events took place.

_____ a. NASA was created.

_____ b. *Sputnik* was launched.

_____ c. The U.S. government funded loans for science students.

4. **Making Correct Inferences**

Two of the statements below are correct *inferences,* or reasonable guesses. They are based on information in the passage. The other statement is an incorrect, or faulty, inference. Label the statements C for *correct* inference and F for *faulty* inference.

_____ a. Americans believed that they needed better science education to win the space race.

_____ b. Before *Sputnik,* American science teachers did not usually emphasize laboratory work.

_____ c. *Sputnik's* effects on American science education were mostly negative.

5. **Understanding Main Ideas**

One of the statements below expresses the main idea of the passage. One statement is too general, or too broad. The other explains only part of the passage; it is too narrow. Label the statements M for *main idea,* B for *too broad,* and N for *too narrow.*

_____ a. The launch of *Sputnik* led Americans to reform science education.

_____ b. Science education prepares people to be researchers or engineers.

_____ c. *Sputnik* gave the Soviet Union an early lead in the space race.

Correct Answers, Part A _____

Correct Answers, Part B _____

Total Correct Answers _____

Japan, an island country in the northern Pacific Ocean, is located in the midst of three of Earth's tectonic plates. These are huge pieces of Earth's crust that "float" on the partially fluid hot rock in Earth's mantle layer. Two of these plates, the Pacific Plate and the Philippine Plate, are moving toward the third, the Eurasian Plate, and plunging beneath it. Both earthquakes and volcanoes are features associated with plate boundaries. Japan experiences about 15 hundred earthquakes every year and has at least 60 active volcanoes.

On September 1, 1923, the Great Kanto Earthquake struck the Tokyo area. It is estimated that the main quake lasted up to 10 minutes, with two and a half hours of constant trembling. One witness described a "sickening sway" and "vicious grinding of timbers." The quake struck about noon, when many people were cooking lunch over coal stoves. Fires broke out throughout the quake area. Flames quickly consumed Yokohama and burned for two days. From the first shaking on September 1 until the activity died down on September 6, more than 800 smaller quakes—called aftershocks—occurred. In the end, most of Yokohama and one-third of Tokyo were destroyed, and more than 142 thousand people were dead.

The Great Hanshin Earthquake struck near Kobe on January 17, 1995. This quake caused almost 5,300 deaths and destroyed or seriously damaged about 241 thousand houses. As in the case of the Kanto earthquake, many of the deaths were a result of fires, but falling debris also took its toll. Traditional Japanese houses are made of wood frames topped with heavy clay-and-tile roofs. These buildings withstand fierce typhoons but not the shaking that occurs during strong earthquakes.

Between 1991 and 1995, the Unzen volcano erupted often. Heavy rains loosened debris on the slopes. This caused landslides. Hundreds of houses were destroyed, dozens of people died, and thousands had to leave.

Earthquakes, volcanoes, and landslides may cause harmful ocean waves called tsunamis. Tsunamis begin when Earth movements set ocean water into motion. In the open ocean, tsunamis are harmless and even undetectable. When they approach shallow water close to land, however, the water piles up, creating a wave between 30 and 100 feet high. An eruption of the Unzen volcano in 1792 caused a landslide and a tsunami that killed some 15 thousand people. Disastrous tsunamis also struck Japan in 1883, 1896, 1983, and 1993.

Reading Time _____

Recalling Facts

1. Huge pieces of Earth's crust are called
   - ❏ a. timbers.
   - ❏ b. tsunamis.
   - ❏ c. tectonic plates.

2. The Great Kanto Earthquake caused great destruction to the cities of
   - ❏ a. Kobe and Yokohama.
   - ❏ b. Tokyo and Yokohama.
   - ❏ c. Kobe, Tokyo, and Yokohama.

3. The three plates that interact to form the Japanese islands are
   - ❏ a. the Asian, Philippine, and Pacific plates.
   - ❏ b. the Japan, Philippine, and Pacific plates.
   - ❏ c. the Eurasian, Philippine, and Pacific plates.

4. In 1792 an eruption of the Unzen volcano led to
   - ❏ a. a tsunami that killed some 15 thousand people.
   - ❏ b. 5 thousand deaths.
   - ❏ c. fires that destroyed most of Yokohama.

5. When heavy rains loosen material on the slopes of volcanoes, the result is
   - ❏ a. a landslide.
   - ❏ b. a tsunami.
   - ❏ c. an earthquake.

Understanding Ideas

6. If the Great Kanto Earthquake had occurred in the middle of the night,
   - ❏ a. a tsunami would have occurred.
   - ❏ b. fewer fires probably would have started.
   - ❏ c. more buildings would have collapsed in the aftershocks.

7. An inference that can be drawn from the passage is that, compared with earthquakes, volcanic eruptions
   - ❏ a. occur less often.
   - ❏ b. give more advance warning.
   - ❏ c. are more likely to cause a tsunami.

8. Tsunamis are destructive only when they
   - ❏ a. reach land.
   - ❏ b. coincide with landslides.
   - ❏ c. encounter ships in the open ocean.

9. The passage suggests that the collapsing of traditional Japanese houses during earthquakes is chiefly a result of
   - ❏ a. fires.
   - ❏ b. aftershocks.
   - ❏ c. their timber and tile-roof construction.

10. Compared with temperatures at Earth's surface, temperatures in the mantle are
    - ❏ a. lower.
    - ❏ b. higher.
    - ❏ c. the same.

Japan is one of Earth's major archipelagos, or large island groups. Others include Hawaii, the Galapagos Islands, and the islands of the South Pacific. Although the origins vary, the islands that make up archipelagos were all formed the same way.

Many archipelagos were formed by undersea volcanoes. When such volcanoes erupt, lava hardens and builds up. In due course, it rises above the surface to form an island. The volcanoes that formed Japan arose from the meeting of three tectonic plates. Ironically, the earthquakes, volcanoes, and tsunamis that buffet Japan are the consequence of the same forces.

The volcanoes that formed the Hawaiian group resulted from hot spots—stationary plumes of magma, a molten-rock mixture, that form near a heat source in Earth's mantle. As a plate floats over a hot spot, the magma rises through the crust. An island is formed, and volcanic activity slowly fades as the plate moves away. The Galapagos Islands, known for their unique wildlife, were also formed in this manner.

Many of the islands that make up the South Pacific archipelagos are coral islands, which begin as volcanic islands. Coral reefs grow around the islands. Over time the islands sink, or the water rises. The original islands disappear, but the coral reefs continue to grow until only circular reefs, called atolls, remain.

1. **Recognizing Words in Context**

Find the word *buffet* in the passage. One definition below is closest to the meaning of that word. One definition has the opposite or nearly the opposite meaning. The remaining definition has a completely different meaning. Label the definitions C for *closest,* O for *opposite or nearly opposite,* and D for *different.*

_____ a. miss

_____ b. pound

_____ c. serve

2. **Distinguishing Fact from Opinion**

Two of the statements below present *facts,* which can be proved. The other statement is an *opinion,* which expresses someone's thoughts or beliefs. Label the statements F for *fact* and O for *opinion.*

_____ a. Coral islands often originate as volcanic islands.

_____ b. The same forces that created the Japanese islands also cause destruction.

_____ c. The Galapagos Islands make up the most valuable archipelago because of the unique wildlife there.

3. Keeping Events in Order

Number the statements below 1, 2, and 3 to show the order in which the events took place.

_____ a. At a hot spot, magma rises through the crust as a volcano.

_____ b. An island is formed.

_____ c. The plate moves away from the hot spot, and the volcanic activity gradually ceases.

4. Making Correct Inferences

Two of the statements below are correct *inferences,* or reasonable guesses. They are based on information in the passage. The other statement is an incorrect, or faulty, inference. Label the statements C for *correct* inference and F for *faulty* inference.

_____ a. Islands that make up an archipelago have similar geography.

_____ b. Because the Hawaiian and Galapagos island groups were both formed from hot spots, they probably have similar environments.

_____ c. Not all volcanic islands are formed from the same tectonic conditions.

5. Understanding Main Ideas

One of the statements below expresses the main idea of the passage. One statement is too general, or too broad. The other explains only part of the passage; it is too narrow. Label the statements M for *main idea*, B for *too broad*, and N for *too narrow.*

_____ a. Some volcanic islands have formed near hot spots.

_____ b. The islands that make up individual archipelagos were all formed in the same way, often as a result of undersea volcanoes.

_____ c. Archipelagos are found throughout the world's oceans.

Correct Answers, Part A _____

Correct Answers, Part B _____

Total Correct Answers _____

The Tension Between Free Enterprise and Government Regulation

The expression "robber barons" was first used by Matthew Josephson, a social critic. It referred to some wealthy businessmen who made their fortunes in the late 1800s. Josephson pointed out that these men were becoming as powerful as feudal lords. However, feudal lords had protected their subjects. The robber barons got rich by exploiting their workers without regard for the workers' welfare.

Many historians now credit these tycoons with making America a great industrial nation. They built the railroads that connected the East and West coasts. They provided the coal and other resources that powered factories. Their methods, however, were ruthless. They used their control of resources such as coal to keep prices high. Their large companies forced smaller ones out of business. Children as young as six worked all day in their mines and their factories.

These excesses made people see the need to set some limits on free enterprise. In 1887 Congress established a federal agency to control the railroads. That agency, the Interstate Commerce Commission, was the first that had the power to make rules for private businesses. Today, more than 100 regulatory agencies can make rules.

Many of these agencies were formed to protect the public. The Occupational Health and Safety Administration makes rules for safety on the job. The Food and Drug Administration decides which drugs are safe to use and protects the food supply.

Other agencies ensure fair competition. The Federal Trade Commission (FTC) keeps companies from agreeing to charge the same price for their goods. The FTC must also review and approve mergers that might give one company too much control of an industry.

At first government agencies had only narrow powers. Then concern grew over problems that can affect more than one industry, such as pollution. After the Environmental Protection Agency was formed to watch for problems that affect the environment, other agencies with broad powers were set up in the 1980s. At the same time, some industries were "deregulated" (rules affecting airlines and utilities were eased).

Debate over regulation goes on. In 1999 it cost businesses more than $750 billion to follow federal guidelines. Some say that these rules are a great burden on the economy. Others say that the collapse of giant companies such as Enron and WorldCom shows the need for tighter rules.

Reading Time _____

Recalling Facts

1. Critics called the wealthy business-men who built the railroads
   - ❏ a. "land pirates."
   - ❏ b. "robber barons."
   - ❏ c. "American dukes."

2. The first government regulatory agency was set up to
   - ❏ a. end child labor.
   - ❏ b. reduce competition.
   - ❏ c. regulate the railroads.

3. Today the number of agencies that can make rules for private businesses is
   - ❏ a. fewer than 10.
   - ❏ b. more than 100.
   - ❏ c. between 40 and 50.

4. The agency that sets standards for job safety is the
   - ❏ a. Federal Trade Commission.
   - ❏ b. Food and Drug Administration.
   - ❏ c. Occupational Health and Safety Administration.

5. One government agency with power over several industries is the
   - ❏ a. National Park Service.
   - ❏ b. Environmental Protection Agency.
   - ❏ c. Federal Communications Commission.

Understanding Ideas

6. The history of the robber barons suggests that government regulation
   - ❏ a. stifled the growth of the railroads.
   - ❏ b. can become the problem instead of the solution.
   - ❏ c. is needed to protect the public from ruthless business executives.

7. One can conclude that Americans believe that business owners should
   - ❏ a. run their businesses as they see fit.
   - ❏ b. make a profit without hurting the public.
   - ❏ c. work only for the public good, not for profit.

8. Compared with the first government regulatory agencies, those of today have
   - ❏ a. fewer powers.
   - ❏ b. broader powers.
   - ❏ c. about the same powers.

9. Efforts to deregulate some industries show that Americans
   - ❏ a. want no more regulation than is necessary.
   - ❏ b. believe that some industries can regulate themselves.
   - ❏ c. agree that government regula-tion is the solution to most problems.

10. The passage shows how Americans have
    - ❏ a. resisted government rules.
    - ❏ b. adopted government ownership of major industries.
    - ❏ c. tried to encourage free enterprise while protecting the public.

18 ⬛ B   Food from the 'Hood

In 1992, students at Crenshaw High School turned a garden into a business. Food from the 'Hood began as a response to violent Los Angeles riots. One cause of the riots was the verdict in the Rodney King trial, in which an all-white jury acquitted four police officers accused of beating an African American man. The students also saw another reason for the riots: lack of economic opportunity.

The students responded by forming their own natural-foods business. A teacher and a volunteer adviser helped them make a plan. In October, the student-owners planted crops in a garden behind the school. By late December, they had donated their first harvest to a neighborhood food bank.

The next year, they developed their quarter-acre garden into a business asset. They sold their produce at a local farmer's market. They also started a line of salad dressings. Half of the profits were used to expand their company. The rest went into a scholarship fund.

Today students still learn business skills by managing Food from the 'Hood. They give one-quarter of their produce to the needy. Their products bring in $250 thousand a year.

As students expand the company, they also cultivate their futures. More than 70 students who were once at risk of dropping out have gone on to college.

1. **Recognizing Words in Context**

   Find the word *acquitted* in the passage. One definition below is closest to the meaning of that word. One definition has the opposite or nearly the opposite meaning. The remaining definition has a completely different meaning. Label the definitions C for *closest*, O for *opposite or nearly opposite*, and D for *different*.

   _____ a. discussed

   _____ b. punished

   _____ c. absolved

2. **Distinguishing Fact from Opinion**

   Two of the statements below present *facts*, which can be proved. The other statement is an *opinion*, which expresses someone's thoughts or beliefs. Label the statements F for *fact* and O for *opinion*.

   _____ a. Food from the 'Hood helps student-owners go to college.

   _____ b. Food from the 'Hood salad dressings are the best on the market.

   _____ c. Food from the 'Hood helps students acquire business skills.

3. **Keeping Events in Order**

Number the statements below 1, 2, and 3 to show the order in which the events took place.

_____ a. Riots broke out in Los Angeles.

_____ b. Crenshaw students founded Food from the 'Hood.

_____ c. Four Los Angeles police officers accused of beating an African American man were acquitted.

4. **Making Correct Inferences**

Two of the statements below are correct *inferences*, or reasonable guesses. They are based on information in the passage. The other statement is an incorrect, or faulty, inference. Label the statements C for *correct* inference and F for *faulty* inference.

_____ a. If high school students run a business, it will be profitable.

_____ b. No pesticides are used in the Food from the 'Hood garden.

_____ c. Students have developed a line of Food from the 'Hood products.

5. **Understanding Main Ideas**

One of the statements below expresses the main idea of the passage. One statement is too general, or too broad. The other explains only part of the passage; it is too narrow. Label the statements M for *main idea*, B for *too broad*, and N for *too narrow*.

_____ a. Student-run businesses can be valuable to a community.

_____ b. Some Food from the 'Hood produce is given to the needy.

_____ c. Food from the 'Hood is a successful student-run business.

Correct Answers, Part A _____

Correct Answers, Part B _____

Total Correct Answers _____

The Emancipation Proclamation: "A Fit and Necessary War Measure"

In 1862 the Civil War was going badly for the North. President Abraham Lincoln knew that he must take action. The Emancipation Proclamation, issued on January 1, 1863, was his way of adding new meaning to the struggle. The document declared that all enslaved persons in states and territories in active rebellion against the United States would from that day on be free.

In private life, Lincoln had always been against slavery. As president, however, his first priorities were to uphold the Constitution and preserve the Union. Before the South actively rebelled against the United States, Lincoln took a middle ground in his policy toward slavery. During his campaign, he promised to "take no actions as president to impair or limit slavery in those states where it existed." By 1861 all 11 Southern states had seceded from the Union. The Civil War had begun. From the start, the foremost aim of the North was to hold the United States together. Lincoln feared that the four border states, which were proslavery but also pro-Union, would join the Confederacy. Thus, he was careful to assume a neutral stance on the issue.

As the war raged on, Lincoln saw that he could not maintain this stance. Union battle losses had piled up. The U.S. armed forces also were suffering shortages of men. Lincoln decided that freeing the enslaved people had finally become a "military necessity." Ironically, the Proclamation did not actually free anybody. Because the document applied only to the Confederate states, the United States could free people in the South only by means of victories. However, it turned the tide of the war. Enslaved people fled from their owners in the South and headed north. As a result, a valuable labor force shifted from the South to the North. The Emancipation Proclamation also opened the U.S. armed forces to African American recruits. About 200 thousand African Americans fought for the Union.

Perhaps most important, the proclamation expanded the meaning of the Civil War. The war had become a battle not only to preserve the United States but also to end slavery. As a result, the South could no longer hope for the support of its chief trading partners, Great Britain and France. Both countries opposed slavery. The tide of battle shifted, and in April of 1865 the South surrendered. On December 18, 1865, the 13th Amendment to the Constitution outlawed slavery throughout the United States.

Reading Time _____

Recalling Facts

1. The Emancipation Proclamation was issued
   - ❑ a. on January 1, 1863.
   - ❑ b. in the summer of 1862.
   - ❑ c. on December 18, 1865.

2. In his campaign for the presidency, Lincoln promised that he would
   - ❑ a. preserve the Union at any cost.
   - ❑ b. free enslaved persons throughout the United States.
   - ❑ c. not limit or impair slavery in areas where it already existed.

3. Slavery was outlawed everywhere in the United States
   - ❑ a. by the 13th Amendment.
   - ❑ b. at the start of the Civil War.
   - ❑ c. as a result of the Emancipation Proclamation.

4. The United States' original purpose in fighting the Civil War was to
   - ❑ a. end slavery.
   - ❑ b. preserve the Union.
   - ❑ c. weaken the South's economy.

5. The Civil War broke out as a result of
   - ❑ a. the North's freeing of enslaved people.
   - ❑ b. all 11 Southern states' seceding from the Union.
   - ❑ c. the United States armed forces' opening fighting units to African American volunteers.

Understanding Ideas

6. The Emancipation Proclamation weakened the South by
   - ❑ a. taking away its labor force.
   - ❑ b. motivating plantation owners to move north.
   - ❑ c. encouraging the border states to remain in the Union.

7. The fact that Lincoln was opposed to slavery and yet did nothing to end it before the Civil War shows that he
   - ❑ a. was a dishonest politician.
   - ❑ b. respected slavery.
   - ❑ c. was willing to put the country's interests first.

8. Lincoln issued the Emancipation Proclamation because he
   - ❑ a. wanted to free enslaved people.
   - ❑ b. wanted to remain neutral on the question of slavery.
   - ❑ c. believed that freeing enslaved persons would benefit the North.

9. One can infer from this passage that
   - ❑ a. without the Emancipation Proclamation, the South might have won the Civil War.
   - ❑ b. the 13th Amendment repeated the Emancipation Proclamation.
   - ❑ c. the Emancipation Proclamation was an empty gesture.

10. Which of the following best supports the idea that the Emancipation Proclamation was a war strategy?
    - ❑ a. Lincoln did not end slavery until the North started losing.
    - ❑ b. The South was willing to go to war to support slavery.
    - ❑ c. The Emancipation Proclamation allowed African American soldiers to serve in the military.

The Fighting 54th

The Emancipation Proclamation permitted free African Americans and former enslaved people to join the U.S. armed forces. Several African American regiments were formed. Perhaps the most famous of these was the 54th Massachusetts Infantry. The troop consisted of about one thousand soldiers. Five months after the Proclamation, the soldiers were ready to fight. Twenty-five-year-old Captain Robert Gould Shaw was promoted to colonel. He commanded the 54th.

One of the regiment's first assignments was to burn and loot the small town of Darien, Georgia. Shaw complained that this was beneath the dignity of his men. He stressed the importance of African American troops' being actively engaged in battle. As a result, the regiment was ordered to South Carolina, where Union troops were fighting to capture the small islands that protected Charleston Harbor. On July 18, 1863, the 54th mounted an attack on heavily fortified Fort Wagner. Under heavy fire, Colonel Shaw led his men up the sloped, sandbagged walls of the fort. Shaw was killed as he reached the top. In all, 281 members of the 54th died that day.

Although the attack was unsuccessful and Fort Wagner remained in Confederate control, the 54th gained distinction for its bravery and skill. A massive bronze sculpture on the Boston Common stands as a memorial. The film *Glory* tells the story.

1. **Recognizing Words in Context**

   Find the word *mounted* in the passage. One definition below is closest to the meaning of that word. One definition has the opposite or nearly the opposite meaning. The remaining definition has a completely different meaning. Label the definitions C for *closest*, O for *opposite or nearly opposite*, and D for *different*.

   _____ a. thwarted

   _____ b. began

   _____ c. ended

2. **Distinguishing Fact from Opinion**

   Two of the statements below present *facts*, which can be proved. The other statement is an *opinion*, which expresses someone's thoughts or beliefs. Label the statements F for *fact* and O for *opinion*.

   _____ a. The 54th Massachusetts is a famous African American Civil War regiment.

   _____ b. Colonel Robert Gould Shaw believed that looting and burning was beneath the dignity of his troops.

   _____ c. The movie *Glory* is not worthwhile.

87

3. **Keeping Events in Order**

Number the statements below 1, 2, and 3 to show the order in which the historical events took place.

_____ a. Shaw and 280 of his men were killed.

_____ b. The 54th Massachusetts regiment was formed.

_____ c. The Emancipation Proclamation was issued.

4. **Making Correct Inferences**

Two of the statements below are correct *inferences,* or reasonable guesses. They are based on information in the passage. The other statement is an incorrect, or faulty, inference. Label the statements C for *correct* inference and F for *faulty* inference.

_____ a. Shaw respected the soldiers under his command.

_____ b. A regiment can lose a battle and still be considered heroic.

_____ c. The soldiers of the 54th Massachusetts regiment were braver than the Confederate soldiers who defended Fort Wagner.

5. **Understanding Main Ideas**

One of the statements below expresses the main idea of the passage. One statement is too general, or too broad. The other explains only part of the passage; it is too narrow. Label the statements M for *main idea,* B for *too broad,* and N for *too narrow.*

_____ a. About one thousand African American soldiers made up the 54th Massachusetts regiment.

_____ b. The 54th Massachusetts regiment showed that African American soldiers could make an important contribution to the North's war effort.

_____ c. After the Emancipation Proclamation, African American soldiers fought in the Civil War.

Correct Answers, Part A _____

Correct Answers, Part B _____

Total Correct Answers _____

The Cold War: A Clash of Superpowers

At the start of the twenty-first century, the United States was arguably the only global superpower. However, in the second half of the twentieth century, the United States "shared" center stage with another superpower. Its relationship with the Union of Soviet Socialist Republics, or USSR, though, was anything but cooperative. Instead, the two countries waged a war of nerves known as the Cold War.

As the rest of the world watched with fear, these two superpowers fought for supremacy without ever actually going to war. The weapons they built and stored, but never used, were nuclear. As each side's arsenal grew, the other added to its own stockpile. At the height of this arms race, each side was capable of killing every living thing on Earth.

The Cold War began in the wake of World War II. In that conflict, the United States and the USSR had fought as allies, along with Britain and France, against Nazi Germany. Soon after Hitler's defeat in May of 1945, the alliance fell apart. Two years later, the battle lines were drawn. The democratic capitalist governments of the West feared and mistrusted the Communist government of the USSR. In turn the Communists considered the capitalists decadent and imperialistic. The Soviets installed puppet governments in Eastern Europe. The United States and its European allies joined to form the North Atlantic Treaty Organization to combat the spread of communism in Europe.

In October of 1962, the two superpowers stood on the brink of war. At issue were missile sites secretly being built by the Soviet Union in Cuba. Then-president John F. Kennedy declared that he would turn back ships en route from the Soviet Union if Soviet Premier Nikita Khrushchev did not recall them. The world held its breath as the threat of all-out nuclear war seemed very real, but Khrushchev backed down, and the Cuban missile crisis ended.

After that, tensions eased. Both sides sought to limit the spread of nuclear weapons (culminating in the SALT talks of 1972). They then began to dismantle existing nuclear weapons. The Cold War ended in the autumn of 1990 with the signing of the Charter of Paris for a New Europe. In part it declared that the "era of confrontation and division in Europe has ended." The anti-Communist movements that had gained power throughout the 1980s brought about the dissolution of the Soviet Union, which officially ceased to exist on December 25, 1991.

Reading Time _____

Recalling Facts

1. Which of the following countries was not a U.S. ally during World War II?
   - ❏ a. France
   - ❏ b. Germany
   - ❏ c. the Soviet Union

2. The Cold War was between
   - ❏ a. world democracy and world communism.
   - ❏ b. Germany and the United States.
   - ❏ c. the United States and the Soviet Union.

3. The highly tense series of events that marked the turning point of the Cold War was the
   - ❏ a. SALT talks.
   - ❏ b. Cuban missile crisis.
   - ❏ c. Charter of Paris for a New Europe.

4. The weapons of the Cold War were particularly terrifying because they
   - ❏ a. were nuclear.
   - ❏ b. existed in huge numbers.
   - ❏ c. were near the United States.

5. The North Atlantic Treaty Organization was organized in response to the
   - ❏ a. arms race.
   - ❏ b. defeat of Nazi Germany in May of 1945.
   - ❏ c. spread of Soviet-controlled governments.

Understanding Ideas

6. Given its context in the passage, SALT probably stands for
   - ❏ a. superpower alert, level two.
   - ❏ b. secret aim liquidation tactics.
   - ❏ c. strategic arms limitation talks.

7. The author uses "arguably" in the first sentence because
   - ❏ a. she is angry.
   - ❏ b. most, but not all, people would agree with her.
   - ❏ c. no one agrees on the definition of *superpower*.

8. It is evident from the passage that a puppet government is
   - ❏ a. communist.
   - ❏ b. under the control of another government.
   - ❏ c. a weak regime that tries to imitate the behaviors of a stronger regime.

9. President Kennedy probably learned of the missile sites from
   - ❏ a. spy missions.
   - ❏ b. Cuban leaders.
   - ❏ c. television and radio.

10. It is reasonable to assume that Premier Khrushchev retreated because
    - ❏ a. his government was weak.
    - ❏ b. he was afraid of President Kennedy.
    - ❏ c. he was unwilling to engage in a nuclear war.

When the Cold War Crumbled

The Berlin Wall was a prime symbol of the Cold War. It was built in a divided city in a divided country in a world essentially divided between democracy and communism.

After World War II, France, Britain, the United States, and the Soviet Union split Germany into four zones. Berlin, which lay in the Soviet zone, was also split. As the alliance between the West and the Soviets ended, Germany emerged as two entities—democratic West Germany and communist East Germany.

In the aftermath, more than two million East Germans fled to West Germany. Alarmed by the loss of so many skilled workers, East Germany built the Berlin Wall in August of 1961 to stop the flow. By the 1980s, the wall was fortified and armed. It extended some 100 miles. East Germans continued to make it through, though many were caught and arrested. Almost 200 East Germans were killed.

In 1989 the East German leadership was ousted by the anti-Communist movement sweeping through Europe. Crowds collected at the wall in early November. On the night of November 9, West Germans scaled the wall, reached down to their Eastern neighbors, and pulled them over. Then, armed with hand tools, united German citizens began chipping away. At the stroke of midnight, the wall, hated symbol of the Cold War, came tumbling down.

1. **Recognizing Words in Context**

   Find the word *ousted* in the passage. One definition below is closest to the meaning of that word. One definition has the opposite or nearly the opposite meaning. The remaining definition has a completely different meaning. Label the definitions C for *closest,* O for *opposite or nearly opposite,* and D for *different.*

   _____ a. removed from office

   _____ b. revealed to the public

   _____ c. elected to office

2. **Distinguishing Fact from Opinion**

   Two of the statements below present *facts,* which can be proved. The other statement is an *opinion,* which expresses someone's thoughts or beliefs. Label the statements F for *fact* and O for *opinion.*

   _____ a. Germany emerged as democratic West Germany and communist East Germany.

   _____ b. The Berlin Wall was the symbol of the Cold War.

   _____ c. The Berlin Wall was erected in a divided city in a divided country.

3. Keeping Events in Order

Number the statements below 1, 2, and 3 to show the order in which the events took place.

_____ a. Germany is divided into four zones.

_____ b. Almost 200 East Germans are killed while trying to cross into West Germany.

_____ c. The Berlin Wall is built by East Germany to stop emigration to the West.

4. Making Correct Inferences

Two of the statements below are correct *inferences,* or reasonable guesses. They are based on information in the passage. The other statement is an incorrect, or faulty, inference. Label the statements C for *correct* inference and F for *faulty* inference.

_____ a. Many East Germans preferred to live in the West.

_____ b. Germany was divided into zones because the allies did not trust one another.

_____ c. The German citizens wanted the wall to come down at a particular moment.

5. Understanding Main Ideas

One of the statements below expresses the main idea of the passage. One statement is too general, or too broad. The other explains only part of the passage; it is too narrow. Label the statements M for *main idea,* B for *too broad,* and N for *too narrow.*

_____ a. The Berlin Wall stopped East Germans from emigrating.

_____ b. During the Cold War, the world was basically divided between democracy and communism.

_____ c. The Berlin Wall and its rise and fall symbolized the Cold War.

Correct Answers, Part A _____

Correct Answers, Part B _____

Total Correct Answers _____

Jury Duty, Jury Rights

Most people think of jury service as a duty of citizenship. But it also can be viewed as a right. According to the U.S. Constitution, deciding guilt or innocence is not the only function of trial by jury. In a criminal trial, a jury also can refuse to apply a law. However, some people believe that jurors are taking this right too far.

In a criminal trial, the state presents evidence of the defendant's guilt, and the defense tries to show that the defendant is not guilty. The jury weighs the evidence and comes to a verdict that must be unanimous—that is, all 12 jurors must agree. If even a single juror votes in opposition to the others, the case ends in a mistrial. For the state to get a conviction, it must retry the defendant.

A juror may have reasons for voting against the other jurors. The juror in question may honestly think that the evidence does not support a conviction. On the other hand, the juror may believe that the law itself is unjust or that it is being applied unfairly. The juror may believe that the defendant is not guilty according to those grounds. This practice, called jury nullification, can be traced back to colonial days. In 1735 newspaper publisher John Peter Zenger was tried for libel for printing criticisms of New York's governor. At the time, it was illegal to criticize the British king or his appointed officials publicly, but the jury acquitted Zenger.

The U.S. Supreme Court has upheld the right of jury nullification, and the practice has indeed been an important force in protesting unjust laws. The Zenger case, for example, established that published criticisms could not be considered libel if they were true. In this case, jury nullification reflected the values of the public. However, the practice becomes a problem when a single juror acts on strong personal bias. Such a juror may nullify a jury in complete disregard of the law and the evidence, especially in controversial laws, such as those related to gun control.

The percentage of criminal cases ending in mistrial has steadily risen in recent decades. Some legal scholars believe that the legal system is put into peril when only one juror can cause a mistrial because of emotion or bias. Some legal scholars have suggested changing the law to make it no longer necessary for a verdict to be unanimous.

Reading Time _____

Recalling Facts

1. In a criminal trial, the state's job is to prove that the defendant is
   - ❑ a. guilty.
   - ❑ b. not guilty.
   - ❑ c. neither a nor b.

2. If a jury cannot agree on a verdict, the result is
   - ❑ a. acquittal.
   - ❑ b. a mistrial.
   - ❑ c. conviction.

3. John Peter Zenger was tried under
   - ❑ a. libel laws.
   - ❑ b. gun-control laws.
   - ❑ c. fugitive slave laws.

4. The practice of refusing to convict a defendant on the ground that the law is unjust or unfairly applied is called
   - ❑ a. a mistrial.
   - ❑ b. jury nullification.
   - ❑ c. antidefendant bias.

5. In recent years, the number of criminal cases ending in mistrial has
   - ❑ a. steadily increased.
   - ❑ b. decreased to some extent.
   - ❑ c. stayed at about the same level.

Understanding Ideas

6. The right of jury nullification is mainly intended to ensure that
   - ❑ a. more cases end in mistrials.
   - ❑ b. a single juror can have power over an entire jury.
   - ❑ c. the laws are applied in ways that the public believes are just.

7. Zenger's acquittal was a step toward
   - ❑ a. the British king's control.
   - ❑ b. prosecutor's rights.
   - ❑ c. freedom of the press.

8. According to the passage, a criminal trial involving gun control is open to jury nullification because
   - ❑ a. gun-control laws are unclear.
   - ❑ b. people have strong personal opinions about the right to own and carry a gun.
   - ❑ c. guns are a hazard to children.

9. If a case ends in a mistrial,
   - ❑ a. the result is essentially the same as an acquittal.
   - ❑ b. a defendant can still be convicted after another trial.
   - ❑ c. the judge and lawyers know that something is wrong with the law.

10. Ending the requirement that a verdict in a criminal trial must be unanimous probably would reduce jury nullification because
    - ❑ a. it would make it easier to acquit a defendant.
    - ❑ b. single jurors would be bolder about going against the majority.
    - ❑ c. it is less likely that more than one juror would base a decision on personal conviction than on the law.

In a democracy, it is vital to have a court system in which judges are independent. They must be free to interpret the law without regard to public opinion or politics. Not everyone agrees, however, on the best way to achieve this goal.

State judges are appointed by the legislature or the governor. Under this system, officials are free to choose judges who are their allies, even though they may not be the best choices.

Allowing the public to elect its judges avoids this pitfall, but this system brings its own problems. It tends to turn judges into politicians. They become concerned with maintaining their popularity. This can affect their decisions in court. Also, conflicts may arise when they must decide cases involving their contributors. Finally, few voters are fully informed about the honesty or qualifications of candidates for judgeships, so there is no guarantee that the best judges will be elected.

Some people believe that merit selection is best. In this method, when an opening for a judgeship occurs, an independent committee screens candidates. This body forwards to the governor or other official a list of those approved. Then that official makes an appointment from the list. Critics point out, however, that the committee itself is made up of appointees. As a result, appointments may not be truly unbiased.

1. **Recognizing Words in Context**

    Find the word *pitfall* in the passage. One definition below is closest to the meaning of that word. One definition has the opposite or nearly the opposite meaning. The remaining definition has a completely different meaning. Label the definitions C for *closest*, O for *opposite or nearly opposite*, and D for *different*.

    _____ a. benefit

    _____ b. drawback

    _____ c. method

2. **Distinguishing Fact from Opinion**

    Two of the statements below present *facts*, which can be proved. The other statement is an *opinion*, which expresses someone's thoughts or beliefs. Label the statements F for *fact* and O for *opinion*.

    _____ a. Voters need to be better informed about the qualifications of judges.

    _____ b. People disagree on the best method of selecting judges.

    _____ c. In merit selection, the nominating committee lists the candidates that it believes are qualified.

3. Keeping Events in Order

Number the statements below 1, 2, and 3 to show the order in which the events took place.

_____ a. The nominating committee forwards a list of approved candidates to the governor.

_____ b. The governor makes an appointment from a list of approved candidates.

_____ c. The nominating committee screens candidates.

4. Making Correct Inferences

Two of the statements below are correct *inferences,* or reasonable guesses. They are based on information in the passage. The other statement is an incorrect, or faulty, inference. Label the statements C for *correct* inference and F for *faulty* inference.

_____ a. Voters would elect the most qualified judges if only the voters were better informed.

_____ b. An ideal method of selecting judges would be one in which only the most qualified candidates would be chosen.

_____ c. A judge with obligations or ties to an individual or group may be less likely to make fair judgments.

5. Understanding Main Ideas

One of the statements below expresses the main idea of the passage. One statement is too general, or too broad. The other explains only part of the passage; it is too narrow. Label the statements M for *main idea*, B for *too broad*, and N for *too narrow*.

_____ a. Of the three main methods of selecting judges, each has strengths and weaknesses.

_____ b. The ways in which states choose judges vary.

_____ c. Elected officials may sometimes appoint unqualified judges.

Correct Answers, Part A _____

Correct Answers, Part B _____

Total Correct Answers _____

The Haitian Revolution: Casting Out the Caste System

In the late 1780s, the French colony of Saint-Domingue was at the peak of its prosperity. It was the world's leading sugar producer. This Caribbean colony of some 560 thousand persons owed its success to the enslaved people who worked its plantations. The social system was a strict caste system. It used skin color to determine one's place in society.

The people of Saint-Domingue were broadly separated into a white upper class and a black underclass. There were distinctions within these castes, however. At the top of the upper class were the *seigneurs,* or lords. These wealthy, white, slaveholding planters owned the plantations and wielded all the power. Under them were white officials, aligned with the government. They worked to keep the planters in power. Under them were poor whites, such as merchants and overseers, who performed duties for the planters. These poor whites had no real power or wealth, but they did have rights before the law. They considered themselves superior to the black underclass, even those much wealthier than they. At the time, the white upper class numbered about 32 thousand.

At the top of the underclass were some 24 thousand free Africans (nonenslaved persons, including those who had been freed) and free people of mixed race. These freed Africans had no social equality with the white upper class but were frequently landholders of substance, owning one-third of the real estate and one-fourth of the wealth. Although they had no legal rights, they did share in the wealth. At the bottom of the caste system were roughly 500 thousand enslaved people, many newly arrived from Africa. They had no rights, no land, and no money. Without them, however, the colony would have perished.

After the slave rebellion of 1791, led by a former enslaved person named Toussaint Louverture, Saint-Domingue's racist caste system was transformed. By 1801 Louverture had maneuvered his way into ruling a largely self-governing state. His new constitution abolished slavery. It also banned racial discrimination in the civil service. However, his new society was not a democracy. Louverture was ruler for life.

In 1802 France tried to reestablish the slave state of Saint-Domingue, overthrowing Louverture in the process; but his second-in-command, the fierce Jean-Jacques Dessalines, foiled French plans. On January 1, 1804, Dessalines unveiled the new Republic of Haiti, from the name used by the Arawak, the original inhabitants of the island.

Reading Time _____

Recalling Facts

1. The group that made up most of the population in prerevolutionary Saint-Domingue was
   - ❏ a. freed enslaved persons.
   - ❏ b. enslaved persons from Africa.
   - ❏ c. the white upper class.

2. The factor that contributed most to Saint-Domingue's success was
   - ❏ a. slave labor.
   - ❏ b. the sugar crops.
   - ❏ c. the French government that ran the colony.

3. The main difference between the two underclasses in colonial Saint-Domingue was that only one had
   - ❏ a. ever endured slavery.
   - ❏ b. any wealth or property.
   - ❏ c. any legal rights in society.

4. Postcolonial Saint-Domingue was different from a modern democracy in that
   - ❏ a. it had no constitution.
   - ❏ b. it still permitted slavery.
   - ❏ c. its leader was appointed for life.

5. The Republic of Haiti was first ruled by
   - ❏ a. Toussaint Louverture.
   - ❏ b. Jean-Jacques Dessalines.
   - ❏ c. the original inhabitants of the island.

Understanding Ideas

6. It is likely that the French government kept the white planters in power because the planters
   - ❏ a. kept many slaves.
   - ❏ b. were able administrators.
   - ❏ c. shared their wealth with France.

7. The poor whites in Saint-Domingue probably felt superior to wealthier blacks because
   - ❏ a. they expected to become rich in time.
   - ❏ b. wealth was not important on the island.
   - ❏ c. skin color was the overriding principle of the caste system.

8. According to the passage, the best definition of a caste system is
   - ❏ a. a social system with many layers.
   - ❏ b. a social system in which people are either very rich or very poor.
   - ❏ c. a rigid class system in which one's place in society is based on factors that cannot be changed, such as race or birth.

9. It is likely that the poor whites and the black landowners in colonial Saint-Domingue
   - ❏ a. resented one other.
   - ❏ b. felt a sympathy for one another.
   - ❏ c. believed in the value of a classless society.

10. The most likely reason for the new republic's name change was that
    - ❏ a. it was a more familiar name.
    - ❏ b. it was a more appealing name.
    - ❏ c. the old name was associated with colonization and slavery.

Toussaint Louverture, the Sudden Hero

Born in 1743 in Saint-Domingue, François Dominique Toussaint was the son of an educated slave. After he was legally freed in 1777, he reared a family and lived a simple life. Well into middle age, he abruptly met his destiny during the slave revolt of 1791.

Soon after helping his former master to escape, Toussaint joined the revolt. He was dismayed to see how poorly organized the troops were. He began to assemble his own army, training and drilling the men in guerrilla warfare. Two years later, as a highly regarded general, Toussaint added Louverture to his name. This is French for overture or introductory section. The name may well have signaled a new direction in his life.

Louverture was endowed with great vigor and drive. He was a charismatic leader, inspiring love and loyalty. He was determined to end slavery and rule a self-governing country. Louverture outmaneuvered Britain, Spain, and particularly France to achieve this goal.

By 1801 Louverture controlled all of Hispaniola. The following year, the French mounted a huge armed campaign to take back Saint-Domingue, crushing Louverture's forces. Louverture gave up his power on the condition that slavery not be reestablished. His power gone, he was wrongly imprisoned by the French. He died in 1803, a year before the newly renamed Republic of Haiti won independence.

1. **Recognizing Words in Context**

   Find the word *charismatic* in the passage. One definition below is closest to the meaning of that word. One definition has the opposite or nearly the opposite meaning. The remaining definition has a completely different meaning. Label the definitions C for *closest*, O for *opposite or nearly opposite,* and D for *different.*

   _____ a. charming

   _____ b. corrupt

   _____ c. repulsive

2. **Distinguishing Fact from Opinion**

   Two of the statements below present *facts,* which can be proved. The other statement is an *opinion,* which expresses someone's thoughts or beliefs. Label the statements F for *fact* and O for *opinion.*

   _____ a. Louverture relinquished power on the condition that slavery not be reestablished.

   _____ b. Louverture's new name was a better name for his new direction in life.

   _____ c. Louverture was endowed with great energy and drive.

3. Keeping Events in Order

Number the statements below 1, 2, and 3 to show the order in which the events took place.

_____ a. Toussaint Louverture controlled all of Hispaniola.

_____ b. Toussaint added Louverture to his name.

_____ c. The French tried to take back the colony.

4. Making Correct Inferences

Two of the statements below are correct *inferences,* or reasonable guesses. They are based on information in the passage. The other statement is an incorrect, or faulty, inference. Label the statements C for *correct* inference and F for *faulty* inference.

_____ a. The author believes that the French should not have arrested Louverture.

_____ b. The country took a new name because its hero, Toussaint, had taken a new name.

_____ c. Louverture had some concern for his former master.

5. Understanding Main Ideas

One of the statements below expresses the main idea of the passage. One statement is too general, or too broad. The other explains only part of the passage; it is too narrow. Label the statements M for *main idea,* B for *too broad,* and N for *too narrow.*

_____ a. Toussaint Louverture is one of history's heroes.

_____ b. Inspired by a slave revolt, Louverture became a formidable leader who brought about an end to slavery in Haiti.

_____ c. The Republic of Haiti achieved independence the year after its hero died.

Correct Answers, Part A _____

Correct Answers, Part B _____

Total Correct Answers _____

Jefferson and Hamilton: Hate that Shaped a Nation

As two of America's founders, Thomas Jefferson and Alexander Hamilton shared many goals and ideals, yet they strongly disliked one another. This dislike arose from their opposing backgrounds, values, and visions for their new country. Strangely, the more hostile their clashes grew, the more creative a force they became. The battles waged between these two brilliant men helped define the ideas and institutions that shape American life, law, and politics to this day.

Hamilton was a man of humble birth. His father had abandoned the family when he was a boy. Jefferson was born into a landowning family with powerful connections. It was Hamilton, not Jefferson, however, who believed that the country would be best led by a strong central government made up of wealthy aristocrats. He believed that presidents and senators should be elected for life. Jefferson was a passionate advocate for equality. He held that people of all stations should have a say in government. His ideal was a country founded on the needs and virtues of people who lived close to the land. He promoted a small central government. These principles became known as Jeffersonian democracy.

Trouble first brewed when both men served in President George Washington's cabinet. Although the Revolutionary War had ended, Great Britain still held some forts in the Northwest Territories. Jefferson, as secretary of state, wanted to use trade sanctions to force the British out. Hamilton, as secretary of the treasury, did not want to risk losing revenue. His position won out, and no trade restrictions were imposed.

The men's differences reached a peak over Hamilton's proposal to set up a national bank. Hamilton supported business interests. He believed that such a bank would help the government regulate its finances. Jefferson was wary of such a plan. He feared that it would give the government too much power, encourage irresponsible use of the nation's money supply, and hurt farmers.

This debate came to include the broader question of the power of the U.S. Constitution. Jefferson pointed out that the Constitution did not expressly permit the formation of a national bank. Therefore, such a bank would be unconstitutional. Hamilton responded that any powers not prohibited by the Constitution would automatically be allowed. This line of reasoning became known as the implied-powers doctrine. Again, Hamilton's views prevailed over Jefferson's. The implied-powers doctrine was upheld by the U.S. Supreme Court and continues to guide lawmaking today.

Reading Time _____

Recalling Facts

1. Alexander Hamilton's childhood was
   - ❏ a. humble.
   - ❏ b. wealthy.
   - ❏ c. aristocratic.

2. One of the reasons Jefferson opposed Hamilton's plan for a national bank was that it would
   - ❏ a. harm the interests of farmers.
   - ❏ b. lead to greater ties with Great Britain.
   - ❏ c. violate the implied-powers doctrine.

3. Thomas Jefferson wanted to expel the British from
   - ❏ a. U.S. banking.
   - ❏ b. military forts.
   - ❏ c. the United States entirely.

4. Under President George Washington, Hamilton served as secretary of
   - ❏ a. war.
   - ❏ b. state.
   - ❏ c. the treasury.

5. The idea that the government retains all powers not specifically denied to it by the Constitution is called
   - ❏ a. federalism.
   - ❏ b. Jeffersonian democracy.
   - ❏ c. the implied-powers doctrine.

Understanding Ideas

6. Hamilton's and Jefferson's views on who should hold governing power in the United States suggest that
   - ❏ a. each man wanted power in the hands of people who shared a background similar to his own.
   - ❏ b. neither man thought that the American people could come together to govern themselves.
   - ❏ c. both men looked beyond their upbringings to form their visions of what was best for America.

7. In matters of relations with Great Britain, Hamilton was probably more willing than Jefferson to
   - ❏ a. violate the Constitution.
   - ❏ b. put trade concerns ahead of national security.
   - ❏ c. seize British property in the United States.

8. Compared with Hamilton's interpretation of the Constitution, Jefferson's was
   - ❏ a. stricter.
   - ❏ b. broader.
   - ❏ c. about the same.

9. The passage supports the idea that conflict between people
   - ❏ a. causes problems beyond personal concerns.
   - ❏ b. chiefly arises from differences in upbringing.
   - ❏ c. can sometimes lead to significant accomplishments.

10. Hamilton probably would have been more likely than Jefferson to support
    - ❏ a. tariffs on imported wheat.
    - ❏ b. tax cuts for large corporations.
    - ❏ c. a welfare system for the needy.

Adam Smith's *Wealth of Nations*

In the history of the United States, the signing of the Declaration of Independence is largely thought to be the most noteworthy event of 1776. Another pivotal advance in thinking, however, took place that same year. *An Inquiry into the Nature and Causes of the Wealth of Nations* was published. Its author, a Scottish philosopher named Adam Smith, is credited as the founder of modern economic theory. Smith was the first thinker to outline the links between social life, politics, and economics.

The book's most enduring concept is the idea of the "invisible hand." Smith made a strong case against government control of the economy. He argued that economic systems form and flourish as a natural result of people's activities. People need to make money, so they work to produce goods that others are willing to buy. Sellers, in turn, use the money they earn to buy goods that they need and want. This pattern of producing, buying, and selling creates a harmonious social system that requires no outside interference by government. It arises naturally—guided, according to Smith, "as if by an invisible hand." Smith's system, now often called free enterprise, forms the basis of modern capitalism as it is known in the United States today.

1. **Recognizing Words in Context**

   Find the word *pivotal* in the passage. One definition below is closest to the meaning of that word. One definition has the opposite or nearly the opposite meaning. The remaining definition has a completely different meaning. Label the definitions C for *closest,* O for *opposite or nearly opposite,* and D for *different.*

   _____ a. essential

   _____ b. insignificant

   _____ c. flawed

2. **Distinguishing Fact from Opinion**

   Two of the statements below present *facts,* which can be proved. The other statement is an *opinion,* which expresses someone's thoughts or beliefs. Label the statements F for *fact* and O for *opinion.*

   _____ a. Many historians credit Adam Smith with founding modern economic theory.

   _____ b. Free enterprise forms the basis of modern capitalism.

   _____ c. An economic system is most harmonious when people are allowed to make their own labor decisions.

3. Keeping Events in Order

Number the statements below 1, 2, and 3 to show the order in which the events took place.

_____ a. People realize that they need to make money.

_____ b. They work to produce goods that others are willing to buy.

_____ c. A harmonious social system is formed.

4. Making Correct Inferences

Two of the statements below are correct *inferences,* or reasonable guesses. They are based on information in the passage. The other statement is an incorrect, or faulty, inference. Label the statements C for *correct* inference and F for *faulty* inference.

_____ a. Smith's "invisible hand" might be interpreted to mean the power of natural consequences.

_____ b. The need for money and the desire for goods encourage people to work.

_____ c. Smith's *An Inquiry into the Nature and Causes of the Wealth of Nations* was inspired by the Declaration of Independence.

5. Understanding Main Ideas

One of the statements below expresses the main idea of the passage. One statement is too general, or too broad. The other explains only part of the passage; it is too narrow. Label the statements M for *main idea,* B for *too broad,* and N for *too narrow.*

_____ a. The economic theories outlined in *An Inquiry into the Nature and Causes of the Wealth of Nations* have influenced life in the United States to this day.

_____ b. People naturally work for what they need and want.

_____ c. *An Inquiry into the Nature and Causes of the Wealth of Nations* was published in 1776.

Correct Answers, Part A _____

Correct Answers, Part B _____

Total Correct Answers _____

Beware the Air

Air is a life-giving blend of oxygen, nitrogen, carbon dioxide, and other gases found in nature. It is laced, however, with tens of thousands of syntheically-made chemicals that cause air pollution. The most dangerous air pollutants are lead and particulate matter. These are toxic particles that are tiny enough to float in the air. Sulfur dioxide, ozone, nitrogen oxides, and carbon monoxide are other substances that pollute the air. They are known to cause breathing problems as well as cancer; birth defects; and brain, nerve, and lung damage. As a result, governments worldwide are increasing efforts to reduce air pollution.

Despite their appearance, smoke-belching power plants and factories do not have the most damaging impact on human health. The main source of air pollution is the burning of fossil fuels, such as coal and gasoline. The most harmful pollution comes from cars and trucks. They are close to the ground and packed together in large numbers in urban areas. As a result, their toxic emissions are inhaled more often.

Many efforts to control air pollution focus on motor vehicles. Western countries have laws that limit the amount of pollution new cars can produce. Devices called catalytic converters turn harmful pollutants into safe gases. From the 1960s to the 1990s, the amount of certain pollutants released by U.S.- and Canadian-built cars was cut by 90 to 95 percent. Because there are many more cars on the road today, however, air pollution is actually much worse now than it was 30 years ago.

Developing countries, on the other hand, lag behind in the battle against air pollution. Roads are often crowded with older cars and trucks that produce excessive pollution. To cope with this problem, some countries are asking people to replace old cars with newer models that burn unleaded fuel. However, for many people this is impossible, so governments have started inspection and maintenance (I/M) programs. I/M programs require people to have their cars checked and then to correct any pollution-causing problems. In addition, many governments are banning leaded gas. Catalytic converters in cars are also becoming more widespread.

Slow-moving and idling cars emit more pollution than faster-moving vehicles. Many city governments are exploring ways to ease traffic jams, such as building better roads and improving traffic signals. In addition, governments are trying to get more people to leave their cars at home and use public transportation or bicycles.

Reading Time _____

Recalling Facts

1. The two most dangerous forms of air pollution are
   - ❏ a. ozone and lead.
   - ❏ b. particulate matter and lead.
   - ❏ c. ozone and particulate matter.

2. Catalytic converters reduce vehicle pollution by
   - ❏ a. filtering out particulate matter.
   - ❏ b. removing the lead from gasoline.
   - ❏ c. changing harmful pollutants into safe gases.

3. The source of pollution most hazardous to human health is emissions from
   - ❏ a. factories.
   - ❏ b. power plants.
   - ❏ c. motor vehicles.

4. Compared with 30 years ago, today's air
   - ❏ a. is more polluted.
   - ❏ b. is less polluted.
   - ❏ c. has about the same amount of pollution.

5. Poisonous air pollutants include
   - ❏ a. sulfur dioxide, lead, and oxygen.
   - ❏ b. ozone, nitrogen oxides, and lead.
   - ❏ c. carbon dioxide, nitrogen, and particulate matter.

Understanding Ideas

6. One of the reasons that getting older vehicles off the road reduces pollution is that older vehicles
   - ❏ a. burn leaded fuel.
   - ❏ b. move more slowly.
   - ❏ c. break down more often.

7. The reason that governments are working to reduce air pollution is that
   - ❏ a. cancer rates are rising.
   - ❏ b. air pollution is very harmful to human health.
   - ❏ c. people need a reason to buy new cars and trucks.

8. One can conclude that in developing countries
   - ❏ a. the people do not like to drive new cars.
   - ❏ b. pollution problems are not so severe.
   - ❏ c. people tend to have less money so it is more difficult for them to buy newer cars.

9. Power plants and factories have minimal impact on human health because
   - ❏ a. their emissions are not toxic.
   - ❏ b. fewer people breathe in their emissions than those of vehicles.
   - ❏ c. laws govern emissions from these sources.

10. Which statement below best expresses the main idea?
   - ❏ a. Traffic congestion is one of the chief causes of pollution.
   - ❏ b. Because air pollution is a threat to human health, governments are taking steps to reduce it.
   - ❏ c. Developing countries are lagging behind Western countries in the fight against pollution.

Pedaling Against Pollution

The harmful effects of air pollution from motor vehicles have been well known since the 1960s. Today many environmentalists promote increased use of bicycles. Cycling is an easy and inexpensive way to reduce air pollution in the world's cities. However, a few factors make cycling an imperfect solution.

In order to reap the benefits of bicycle use, people must be willing to give up use of their cars, at least for short trips. Of all of the world's people, those in the United States are the most unwilling to do so. Forty percent of all U.S. trips are two miles or shorter. Still, the United States has the world's lowest rate of bicycle use; in 1990, 87 percent of all trips were made by automobiles. In some large cities in China, by contrast, bicycles account for about 50 percent of all trips. In Beijing the bicycle is the main mode of transportation, although having so many bicycles has presented problems of its own. Riders often do not obey traffic signals. They slow down traffic, actually raising pollution because idling vehicles emit more pollutants than moving ones. China is exploring construction of bicycle tunnels and overpasses, which would not require vehicles to wait for crossing cyclists and would let traffic flow more smoothly.

1. **Recognizing Words in Context**

   Find the word *idling* in the passage. One definition below is closest to the meaning of that word. One definition has the opposite or nearly the opposite meaning. The remaining definition has a completely different meaning. Label the definitions C for *closest*, O for *opposite or nearly opposite*, and D for *different*.

   _____ a. not moving

   _____ b. broken down

   _____ c. making headway

2. **Distinguishing Fact from Opinion**

   Two of the statements below present *facts*, which can be proved. The other statement is an *opinion*, which expresses someone's thoughts or beliefs. Label the statements F for *fact* and O for *opinion*.

   _____ a. Americans will probably never give up their cars.

   _____ b. There are more bicycles on the road in China than there are in any other country.

   _____ c. In the United States, most trips are made by automobile.

3. Keeping Events in Order

Number the statements below 1, 2, and 3 to show the order in which the events took place.

_____ a. The presence of so many bicycles on Chinese streets causes traffic to slow down.

_____ b. Harmful effects of air pollution were recognized.

_____ c. Chinese cities explore the idea of building bicycle tunnels and overpasses.

4. Making Correct Inferences

Two of the statements below are correct *inferences,* or reasonable guesses. They are based on information in the passage. The other statement is an incorrect, or faulty, inference. Label the statements C for *correct* inference and F for *faulty* inference.

_____ a. Bicycle riding would eliminate much of the world's air pollution if more bicycle tunnels and overpasses could be built.

_____ b. Increased use of bicycles is not a perfect solution to the world's air-pollution problem.

_____ c. Most health benefits of bicycle riding today result from exercise.

5. Understanding Main Ideas

One of the statements below expresses the main idea of the passage. One statement is too general, or too broad. The other explains only part of the passage; it is too narrow. Label the statements M for *main idea*, B for *too broad*, and N for *too narrow.*

_____ a. Cycling may reduce air pollution if both people's attitudes and traffic management can be improved.

_____ b. In Beijing the bicycle is the main mode of transportation.

_____ c. Air pollution is a serious health concern throughout the world.

Correct Answers, Part A _____

Correct Answers, Part B _____

Total Correct Answers _____

The Many Battles of World War II Military Women

During World War I (1914–1918), 30 thousand women served in the U.S. Navy, Coast Guard, and Marines with full military rank. Most were nurses. After the United States entered World War II in 1942, the government realized that the armed forces would need the services of even greater numbers of women. By 1943 each branch of the service had a women's corps. Although this meant that new opportunities were now available, the women in the military also faced some problems.

The Navy established the Women Accepted for Volunteer Emergency Service, or WAVES. The army formed the WAC, or Women's Army Corps. Only the Marines did not single women out with their own corps name. Like the men, they were known as Marines. Women pilots also played a crucial role in the war effort. Known as WASPs, or the Women's Air Force Service Pilot corps, they flew a wide variety of noncombatant missions. Unlike the other women's corps, however, they had no military status.

WASPs, WACs, WAVES, and female Marines served in many roles. They were pilots, drivers, parachute riggers, and air-traffic controllers. They served as clerks, nurses, mechanics, and cooks. They filled jobs as radar specialists, code breakers, and radio operators. As freely as the military acknowledged its need for women's skills in wartime, women often found themselves battling an enemy from within—prejudice. This prejudice was shown in numerous ways: Recruiting standards were often much stricter for women than for men. Women, but not men, were sometimes required to be single, speak more than one language, provide references, and have perfect vision. They also had to prove that they had "good moral character."

Educated women and those with unique skills sometimes were assigned to unskilled jobs, such as cooking or baby-sitting for children of high-ranking officers. Rumors that women were inept workers and that they behaved immorally were common. Such talk continued despite official statistics to the contrary. A male soldier, for example, was 150 times more likely to commit an offense under the military code. Army Air Corps studies showed, too, that WASPs had an accident rate of .001 percent, as opposed to male pilots' rate of .007 percent.

The 1948 Women's Armed Services Integration Act made women part of the regular branches of the armed services. Today women serve in all branches of the military with many of the same opportunities as men.

Reading Time _____

Recalling Facts

1. Most of the women who served in the military in World War I worked as
   - ❏ a. nurses.
   - ❏ b. drivers.
   - ❏ c. secretaries.

2. The women's branch of the army was called the
   - ❏ a. WAC.
   - ❏ b. WAVES.
   - ❏ c. WASP corps.

3. The WASP were the only women's corps that did not
   - ❏ a. suffer prejudice.
   - ❏ b. serve in combat roles.
   - ❏ c. have official gender-specific military status.

4. Compared with male pilots, female pilots' error rates were
   - ❏ a. higher.
   - ❏ b. lower.
   - ❏ c. about the same.

5. Separate women's corps in the armed forces were ended in
   - ❏ a. 1943.
   - ❏ b. 1977.
   - ❏ c. 1948.

Understanding Ideas

6. Prejudice against women in the armed services arose because
   - ❏ a. people didn't trust women.
   - ❏ b. the women were working in a traditionally male field.
   - ❏ c. women often lacked the skills necessary to do military jobs.

7. The difference between jobs open to women and to men was that
   - ❏ a. only women served overseas.
   - ❏ b. only men served in combat.
   - ❏ c. women had no military status.

8. The fact that women had to meet higher standards than men in the armed services suggests that
   - ❏ a. the military believed women to be better qualified than men.
   - ❏ b. the military wanted to limit the number of enlisted women.
   - ❏ c. military policy makers believed women not to be equal to men.

9. The fact that military women were often criticized as immoral, even though men were more likely to behave immorally, suggests that
   - ❏ a. women were held to higher standards of morality than men.
   - ❏ b. people did not believe the statistics that proved otherwise.
   - ❏ c. military women were more likely to behave immorally than civilian women were.

10. The main idea of the passage is that
    - ❏ a. women served in many military positions during World War II.
    - ❏ b. World War II made men and women equals for the first time.
    - ❏ c. military women served with skill and honor despite prejudice.

Oveta Culp Hobby: Woman Warrior

Oveta Culp Hobby seemed a woman born to lead. From the age of 20, she held political posts in her native Texas. She ran for the state legislature, married a former Texas governor, and became executive vice president of her husband's paper, the *Houston Post*, before she was 30.

By the time Hobby was in her mid-thirties, she had written a law textbook, become a mother, and served on numerous community and corporate boards. She was a busy person. Therefore, when asked to set up a section on women's activities for the U.S. Army in 1941, Hobby politely refused. However, when her husband said, "You must do whatever your country asks you to do," she took the job.

The Japanese attack on Pearl Harbor in 1941 brought a new army request: assume the command of a newly created women's army corps. Again Hobby demurred, and once more her husband convinced her to reconsider. She accepted the post as head of the Women's Auxiliary Army Corps, or WAAC, with the rank of colonel. She convinced the army to increase the number of jobs open to women and to change the WAAC's status from an auxiliary corps to an army branch. The WAAC was renamed the Women's Army Corps. For her wartime service, Colonel Hobby was awarded the Distinguished Service Medal.

1. Recognizing Words in Context

Find the word *demurred* in the passage. One definition below is closest to the meaning of that word. One definition has the opposite or nearly the opposite meaning. The remaining definition has a completely different meaning. Label the definitions C for *closest,* O for *opposite or nearly opposite,* and D for *different.*

_____ a. declined

_____ b. agreed

_____ c. inclined

2. Distinguishing Fact from Opinion

Two of the statements below present *facts,* which can be proved. The other statement is an *opinion,* which expresses someone's thoughts or beliefs. Label the statements F for *fact* and O for *opinion.*

_____ a. Oveta Culp Hobby worked to raise the status of women in the army.

_____ b. Oveta Culp Hobby owes credit for all her achievements to the support of her husband.

_____ c. Oveta Culp Hobby succeeded at a variety of endeavors at a young age.

3. Keeping Events in Order

Number the statements below 1, 2, and 3 to show the order in which the events took place.

_____ a. The Japanese bombed Pearl Harbor.

_____ b. The WAAC was renamed the WAC.

_____ c. Oveta Culp Hobby wrote a law textbook.

4. Making Correct Inferences

Two of the statements below are correct *inferences,* or reasonable guesses. They are based on information in the passage. The other statement is an incorrect, or faulty, inference. Label the statements C for *correct* inference and F for *faulty* inference.

_____ a. Hobby valued her husband's opinion.

_____ b. Hobby depended on her husband to tell her what to do.

_____ c. Hobby showed more interest in serving her country than in becoming a powerful military figure.

5. Understanding Main Ideas

One of the statements below expresses the main idea of the passage. One statement is too general, or too broad. The other explains only part of the passage; it is too narrow. Label the statements M for *main idea,* B for *too broad,* and N for *too narrow.*

_____ a. Although Oveta Culp Hobby had a full life, she was willing to put aside her personal goals in order to serve her country.

_____ b. Oveta Culp Hobby was a person of many accomplishments.

_____ c. Oveta Culp Hobby attained the rank of colonel in the U.S. Army.

Correct Answers, Part A _____

Correct Answers, Part B _____

Total Correct Answers _____

ANSWER KEY

READING RATE GRAPH

COMPREHENSION SCORE GRAPH

COMPREHENSION SKILLS PROFILE GRAPH

ANSWER KEY

1A   1. c   2. c   3. a   4. b   5. a   6. b   7. b   8. c   9. b   10. b

1B   1. C, D, O   2. F, O, F   3. 3, 1, 2   4. C, C, F   5. B, M, N

2A   1. b   2. b   3. b   4. c   5. b   6. c   7. b   8. c   9. a   10. c

2B   1. C, O, D   2. F, F, O   3. 2, 3, 1   4. C, F, C   5. N, B, M

3A   1. a   2. a   3. b   4. b   5. b   6. c   7. c   8. a   9. a   10. b

3B   1. D, C, O   2. F, O, F   3. 3, 2, 1   4. C, C, F   5. M, N, B

4A   1. c   2. b   3. b   4. c   5. b   6. c   7. b   8. b   9. a   10. a

4B   1. O, D, C   2. F, F, O   3. 2, 1, 3   4. F, C, C   5. B, M, N

5A   1. a   2. a   3. a   4. c   5. c   6. b   7. b   8. a   9. c   10. a

5B   1. D, O, C   2. O, F, F   3. 3, 1, 2   4. C, C, F   5. N, M, B

6A   1. b   2. b   3. a   4. b   5. c   6. b   7. a   8. c   9. c   10. a

6B   1. C, O, D   2. F, F, O   3. 3, 2, 1   4. C, F, C   5. B, M, N

7A   1. c   2. b   3. c   4. b   5. a   6. b   7. c   8. b   9. a   10. b

7B   1. D, O, C   2. O, F, F   3. 2, 3, 1   4. F, C, C   5. N, M, B

8A   1. b   2. c   3. a   4. c   5. a   6. c   7. b   8. b   9. c   10. c

8B   1. C, O, D   2. F, F, O   3. 3, 1, 2   4. C, C, F   5. M, B, N

9A   1. b   2. a   3. b   4. a   5. c   6. b   7. c   8. b   9. b   10. c

9B   1. D, O, C   2. O, F, F   3. 1, 3, 2   4. C, F, C   5. B, N, M

10A   1. c   2. c   3. c   4. a   5. b   6. a   7. b   8. b   9. a   10. b

10B   1. D, C, O   2. F, O, F   3. 1, 2, 3   4. F, C, C   5. N, M, B

11A   1. a   2. c   3. b   4. a   5. c   6. b   7. b   8. c   9. b   10. b

11B   1. O, D, C   2. F, F, O   3. 2, 1, 3   4. C, C, F   5. M, B, N

12A   1. b   2. c   3. b   4. a   5. b   6. c   7. c   8. c   9. b   10. a

12B   1. D, C, O   2. O, F, F   3. 1, 3, 2   4. C, F, C   5. B, N, M

13A   1. c   2. a   3. b   4. b   5. c   6. c   7. b   8. b   9. a   10. c

13B   1. O, D, C   2. F, F, O   3. 3, 1, 2   4. F, C, C   5. N, M, B

14A	1. c	2. b	3. a	4. a	5. c	6. c	7. b	8. c	9. a	10. a
14B	1. O, C, D	2. F, O, F	3. 2, 3, 1	4. C, C, F	5. M, B, N
15A	1. a	2. c	3. b	4. c	5. b	6. b	7. c	8. b	9. a	10. c
15B	1. D, O, C	2. O, F, F	3. 1, 2, 3	4. C, F, C	5. N, B, M
16A	1. b	2. c	3. a	4. b	5. a	6. c	7. a	8. c	9. a	10. c
16B	1. C, D, O	2. F, O, F	3. 2, 1, 3	4. C, C, F	5. M, B, N
17A	1. c	2. b	3. c	4. a	5. a	6. b	7. a	8. a	9. c	10. b
17B	1. O, C, D	2. F, F, O	3. 1, 2, 3	4. C, F, C	5. N, M, B
18A	1. b	2. c	3. b	4. c	5. b	6. c	7. b	8. b	9. a	10. c
18B	1. D, O, C	2. F, O, F	3. 2, 3, 1	4. F, C, C	5. B, N, M
19A	1. a	2. c	3. a	4. b	5. b	6. a	7. c	8. c	9. a	10. a
19B	1. D, C, O	2. F, F, O	3. 3, 2, 1	4. C, C, F	5. N, M, B
20A	1. b	2. c	3. b	4. a	5. c	6. c	7. b	8. b	9. a	10. c
20B	1. C, D, O	2. F, O, F	3. 1, 3, 2	4. C, F, C	5. N, B, M
21A	1. a	2. b	3. a	4. b	5. a	6. c	7. c	8. b	9. b	10. c
21B	1. O, C, D	2. O, F, F	3. 2, 3, 1	4. F, C, C	5. M, B, N
22A	1. b	2. a	3. b	4. c	5. b	6. c	7. c	8. c	9. a	10. c
22B	1. C, D, O	2. F, O, F	3. 2, 1, 3	4. C, F, C	5. B, M, N
23A	1. a	2. a	3. b	4. c	5. c	6. c	7. b	8. a	9. c	10. b
23B	1. C, O, D	2. F, F, O	3. 1, 2, 3	4. C, C, F	5. M, B, N
24A	1. b	2. c	3. c	4. a	5. b	6. a	7. b	8. c	9. b	10. b
24B	1. C, D, O	2. O, F, F	3. 2, 1, 3	4. F, C, C	5. M, N, B
25A	1. a	2. a	3. c	4. b	5. c	6. b	7. b	8. c	9. a	10. c
25B	1. C, O, D	2. F, O, F	3. 2, 3, 1	4. C, F, C	5. M, B, N

READING RATE

Put an X on the line above each lesson number to show your reading time and words-per-minute rate for that lesson.

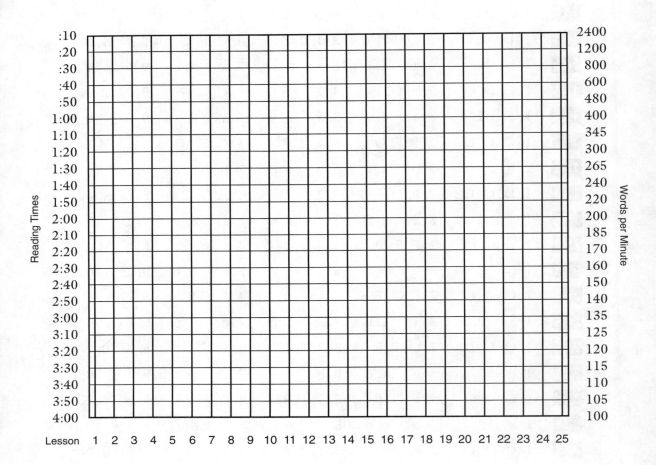

COMPREHENSION SCORE

Put an X on the line above each lesson number to indicate your total correct answers and comprehension score for that lesson.

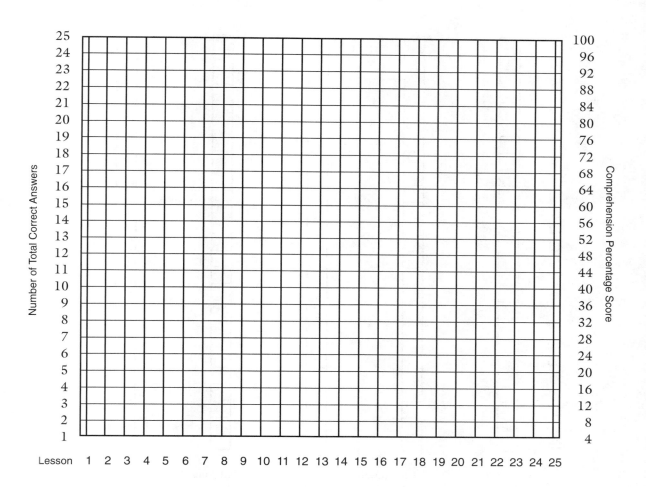

Comprehension Skills Profile

Put an X in the box above each question type to indicate an incorrect reponse to any part of that question.

Lesson	Recognizing Words in Context	Distinguishing Fact from Opinion	Keeping Events in Order	Making Correct Inferences	Understanding Main Ideas
1					
2					
3					
4					
5					
6					
7					
8					
9					
10					
11					
12					
13					
14					
15					
16					
17					
18					
19					
20					
21					
22					
23					
24					
25					